stories of people who
helped build the Great Land

We Alaskans

compiled and edited by
Sharon Bushell

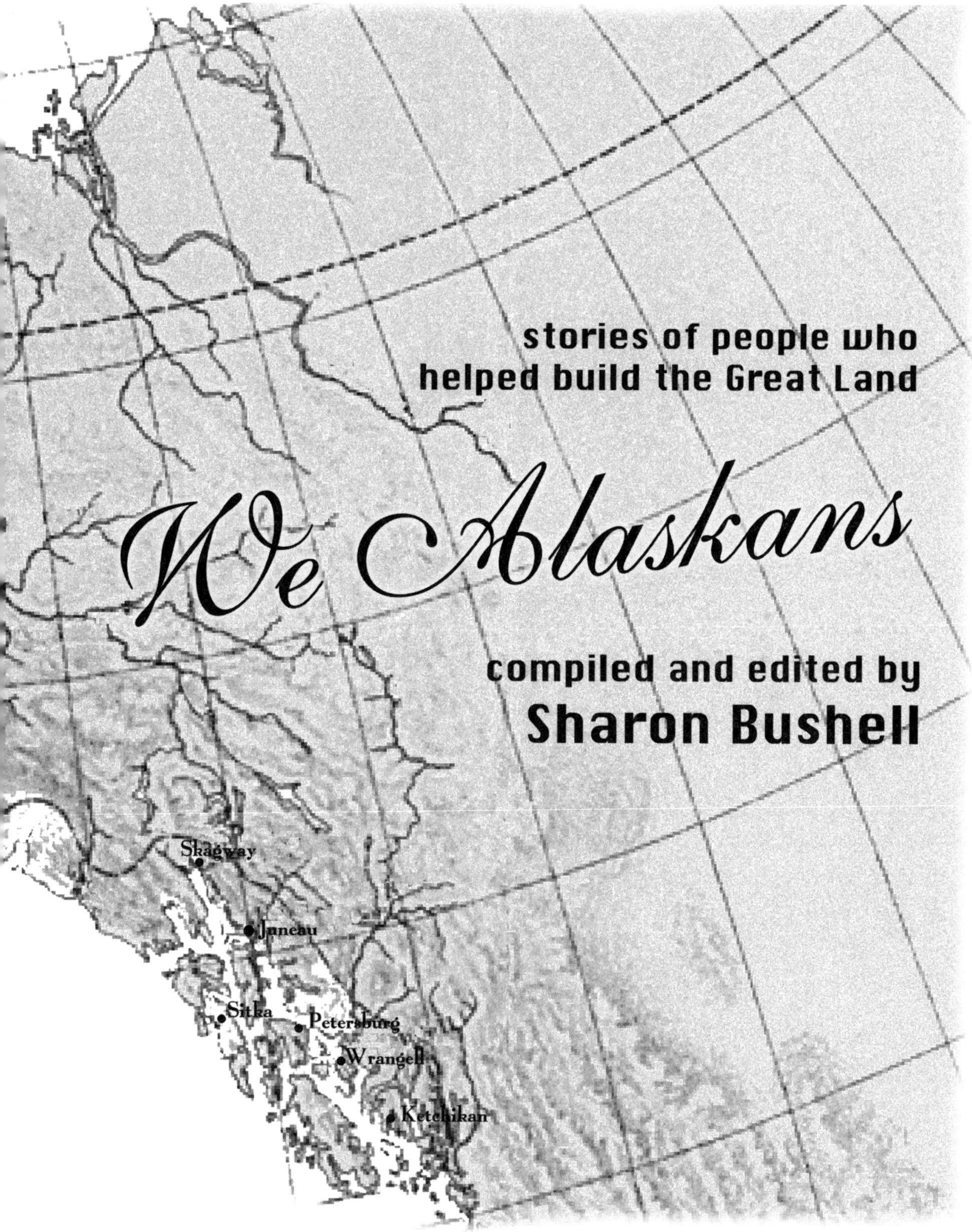

Skagway

Juneau

Sitka Petersburg

Wrangell

Ketchikan

ROAD TUNES MEDIA
534 W. Cowles
Homer, Alaska 99603

Designed by Road Tunes Media
Cover design by Debi Bodett
Manufactured in the United States of America
July 2002
First Edition

10 9 8 7 6 5 4 3 2 1

Library of Congress Cataloging-in-Publication Data
Bushell, Sharon L.
     We Alaskans : Stories of forty-nine people from
the forty-ninth state / Sharon L. Bushell
              p. 219   58 b/w photos.
         1. Alaska - - Biography. 2. Alaska - - History -1900-2002 (20th Century).
I. Title.

979.8
ISBN 0-9721725-0-5   *http://www.wealaskans.com*

We Alaskans

stories of people who
helped build the Great Land

CONTENTS

PREFACE

Like several of the subjects in this book, I had to be dragged north kicking and screaming. I had nothing against Alaska; it's just that I was happy right where I was. But I too had a partner who was insistent about giving Alaska a try, just for a year. After much resistance, I gave in. We bought a beat up '66 Ford station wagon, loaded it to the gills, and headed up the Alcan. As soon as we arrived, like all the subjects in this book, I fell in love with Alaska. That was 25 years ago.

From the beginning, Alaskans intrigued me. There was something unique about them. I couldn't put my finger on it, but it was undeniable. To solve this mystery, I went directly to the source: the old-timers. I asked endless questions, and wouldn't go away until they were answered. My elders indulged me, for they could see that I was hungry for their stories, their humor, their wisdom. They taught me to be in a room and be quiet, to *hear* instead of just listen.

I believe that Alaska's motto, "The Last Frontier," is apt beyond the obvious. The people who left their homes in the 1930s, '40s and '50s to travel to Alaska were truly venturing into the unknown. Like the pioneers who forged their way west in the 19th Century, would-be Alaskans knew little of what awaited them, beyond hardship and toil. Many said goodbye to their families, knowing the chances were good they'd never see them again. Then, almost imperceptibly, the new land became something more than just a place. Going home lost its appeal. They *were* home.

Thanks to the *Anchorage Daily News*, I've been able to share my interest in the lives of elderly Alaskans. The stories contained herein have all been published in the *News*, granting Sunday readers an opportunity to learn more about the old days, about what brought people to this "far flung and desolate place."

I offer my heartfelt thanks to all the people who welcomed me into their homes and shared their stories with me. Not only have their interesting, poignant, humorous tales enhanced my knowledge of things Alaskan, they have defused my fear of aging. Now, rather than dreading the years ahead, I think of them as a challenge. Will I be able to age with the grace and style I have seen in so many "old-timers"? Will I have their wit? Their courage? Maybe. After all, I too am an Alaskan.

Sharon Bushell

Alaska, The Great Land

It must have been the sixth day of the week

and God was genial with an artist's pride,

planning the final touches to His handiwork.

"Today I will create my masterpiece, the ultimate creation.

It will be immense, with soaring mountains

and untrammeled space, to stretch men's souls

and give them room to dream.

I'll pin there the lodestar of the Universe

and the bright spectrum of the Northern Lights

so that once visited, there will be no rest

until men's faces turn again to true north.

I'll make a land to hold them like a lover."

- Mildred Mantle
Anchorage, Alaska

For the man who won my heart at the Talkeetna Moose Dropping Festival in 1981, Johnny B. I tried to resist him, but when he played "Bumble Boogie" I knew that whatever my future held, I wanted him squarely in the center of it. Since then he has enhanced my life in every way imaginable. To him I dedicate this book, for it surely would not have been possible without his tireless effort.

Helen McCrary March

It was my great fortune to meet Helen March in 1984. Our family had just moved to Homer, and the interesting, articulate Mrs. March turned out to be our next-door-neighbor. A lifelong Alaskan, she held me spellbound with tales of her earlier years.

My grandfather came to Alaska in 1900, homesteaded at Copper Center in 1902 and brought his wife and four young sons from California to Valdez in 1904. They traveled by horseback to their home. My father, Nelson, celebrated his tenth birthday by seeing his first snow fall while they camped overnight. As the boys grew they helped clear and plant the land, hauled freight from Valdez north in the winter, hunted and trapped. They also helped their mother, Frances, with the garden and in running the hotel where her good meals were very popular. When the boys were grown and had left home, Frances followed her youngest son, Frank, to Fairbanks, leaving John to continue running a little trading post. At one point he was delivering the mail from Chitina to Gulkana in the winter with a team of horses and a sled on which he had built a covered wagon-type tent with a small wood stove inside to keep him and the contents warm. With lots of water and warm feed, the horses were fine. When the temperature dropped to minus 50 degrees, they often stayed a day or more at a "roadhouse" lodge where there was shelter for the horses and John could get some good food and swap tales.

My mother, Marie Jaakinsen, was about 18 when she left Finland to join a sister in Seattle. Always intrepid, with little money and speaking only Finnish and a little Swedish, she traveled by boat and train with only some minor incidents. She loved to tell about them in later years. She soon found work and by 1910 had joined another sister in Douglas/Juneau. She anglicized her name to Mary Rivers. In 1912 she accepted a job at the Chitina Hotel. While disappointed in the smallness of the community, she forgot all that when she met Nelson. Married in 1913, they were soon running a roadhouse at Dry Creek (now the Gulkana airfield). Their first child was stillborn. When Mary became pregnant again they looked for a doctor. I was born in McCarthy in 1915 at a private home with the doctor from the Kennicott Mine attending. In 10 days Mom and I took the train to Chitina. Dad met us with a horse and buggy to go home to Dry Creek.

In about two years Dad went to work on the Copper River and Northwestern Railroad. I think it was the work train and we lived in one of the cars. I told everyone I was a Finn and, when one of the work crew told my father I should stress the Scots Irish, he defended me and my mother.

Helen March at American Creek, 1940

Fur prices were very high at that time and we next moved to Wooded Island, off the coast of Montague, accompanied by a partner, Floyd Smith. We were to care for the blue foxes, which ran loose on the island. Each fall some were killed. The skins were then shipped to a third partner, who would take care of marketing and banking, with the proceeds to be split three ways. I only remember being afraid the Orca whales would come ashore and eat me as I saw their tall dorsal fins rise and fall in the ocean.

My parents often traveled to Montague with a small boat and what Mom described as an eggbeater-size outboard motor. When it quit in midpassage, Mom rowed while Dad tinkered. On one trip the boat capsized on landing, with Mother caught by the boat before she was clear. I was tumbling in the waves until Floyd caught me by one leg. Mother's large purple hat landed on top of the crossed oars and sailed out in the Pacific. The third partner failed to split the money, and Mother was pregnant with my sister, so next we moved to Latouche, where Dad had been offered a job and I could start school.

In a year we moved back to the Copper River area. I finished second grade in Chitina and met Grandpa John. My father wanted to continue fur farming, so he built us a large log cabin at Pleasant Lake. Mother insisted that her children go to school, even though the Chitina School was 50 miles away. Dad built a small cabin and that year they gave a teacher room and board to teach me. Other years I boarded in Chitina with friends. Grandmother Frances came up from California to take care of my sister, Mary Lee, and me. The little house we rented is still standing. The McCrarys were always friendly and sociable. Wherever we lived there were always picnics and music and dancing, as well as hard work. In the summers we often drove to Kenny Lake Lodge for a Sunday meal. Dad would take his accordion or banjo and play and sing. If there were enough people there was always dancing.

When I finished eighth grade, Mother was determined that I go to high school. So we moved to Cordova and Dad became the fire chief. I was amazed at the sophisticated Cordova high school kids. Much to my mother's horror, I soon gave up wearing gingham dresses and started wearing bell-bottom jeans laced up the back with red sweatshirts, like all the other kids. All 50 of us wore our hip boots to school and let them drag down and go slap! slap! slap! on the floor as we walked. We'd go skating on Lake Eyak, where there were pockets of methane gas that we could light. We'd build a big bonfire on the beach and have hotdogs. We had our school dances in private homes. In the summers we worked in the canneries.

I graduated in 1933 and looked for work. When Dr. Bunnell offered me a summer job at the Alaska Agricultural College and School of Mines College in Fairbanks, I left home, not to return for two years. With a territorial room scholarship and working for my board, college was possible. We were typical college students. We would walk down the street, waking the citizens with our loud songs. We had lots of dances and endless fun.

One day in my senior year, I walked across the frosty campus to kibitz with our cook, Ma Lentz. To warm up a bit, I put my arms around a student who was seated at a coffee table. I had known Jim March (JP) for several years but until that day I had thought he was just a smart aleck with shiny, black, straight hair, and I had little to do with him. I received such a shock after hugging him, I hastily retreated.

I soon changed my mind about a few things. I discovered that he had a wonderful sense of humor. And I learned to love his straight black hair.

I graduated that May from what had become the University of Alaska. I was already employed as secretary to the manager of the Northern Commercial Company. JP and I dated that summer. My parents came up to check him out and approved. We were married October 22, 1937. Our dear friends, Frances and Ray Kohler, stood up for us in the very cold Presbyterian Church. We flew to Circle Hot Springs for a weekend honeymoon. We found a good party going on there. Many people had gathered at the roadhouse to help a miner from Central celebrate his 90th birthday. I'll always remember one fellow doing a Russian dance, squatting on the floor, kicking out one leg and then the other. His balance was pretty good but he kept yelling that he might fall off the floor! We had reserved one of the small cabins, so didn't stay for all of the party. We took a taxi home from the plane in Fairbanks. We just had enough money to pay him.

I had rented a very small apartment. It was just one narrow room with a Murphy bed, a tiny kitchen and a bathroom. When the bed was down there was only room for one chair and a lamp in the corner. But it had city water and was steam heated, as was most of the downtown area. The cockroaches loved that. They could travel all around town on those nice warm pipes.

Jim worked the midnight shift at Fairbanks Exploration Company at Fox. He'd be getting off the bus just as I was walking to work. But in spite of it all, we thought life was just a bowl of cherries. Next spring Jim went to American Creek to be the foreman of the dredging operation. Our friend, Ted Mathews, was the superintendent, and many of the college fellows joined the crew from one year to the next. JP wanted me to spend the summers with him, and my boss allowed me to do that for several years.

The first summer I was the only woman. JP and I lived in a tent on skids, which stuck out in front to form an open deck with a breezy cook space underneath. I stored the canned butter, ham and other other tinned goods there. I cooked on a little "Yukon" stove. It burned wood and had a little bitty oven that held one loaf of bread. It didn't brown on the top, so when the sides were done, I pulled it out and turned it over, often burning my arms or hands. Meat was cooked on top of the stove in a heavy Dutch oven. Running water came from the creek if I chose to run. I thought a home economics course qualified me for anything, though the old miners who often stopped in obviously had their doubts. One time I made a blueberry pie for lunch. Jim took one bite then rushed outdoors to spit it out. I was crushed and wouldn't listen to him until I took a taste. I used unmarked butter tins as cannisters and had put in a cup of salt instead of sugar. It took me quite a while to live that down.

One of those resident miners really wanted to work with the crew. He was about 90 and skinny as a rail. He probably didn't shovel much gravel, but they paid him a little wage and let him ride to the dredge every day with the other workers. I liked that. There were four or five resident miners. They were allowed to eat Sunday dinner at the mess hall for a dollar. After years of scratching for enough flakes of gold and just getting by, they were proud to pay their way and found it a great treat.

When we came off the creek in 1941, we decided to leave Fairbanks and find work for the winter. We stored our belongings with friends and went to Cordova to visit my folks and go duck hunting. While there, we decided to take the first steamship that came by. If it went to Seattle we would be closer to Jim's family. We felt we could both find work. The whole country was gearing up for war. If it went to Seward, fine. Our friends, the Moyers, were there. Roy was working for the Corps of Engineers and we could stay with them. That's how we ended up in Seward for the duration of World War II.

Jim went to work as a rough carpenter on Fort Raymond but was soon put in charge of a group of soldiers surveying and supervising the fortification of Resurrection Bay. Wartime in Seward was exciting. We lived less than a block from anti-aircraft guns. We had gas mask drills. I volunteered with the Red Cross and met with the town fathers, trying to plan how best to evacuate the town in case the Japanese invaded.

Our first son, James Thomas, was born in September 1943. The Corps soon transferred JP to Anchorage, which was a madhouse during the war, with little available housing. Just before our second son, Donald McCrary, was born, JP decided to leave the Corps and become a well driller. He also fished in Bristol Bay in a cannery boat with sails. Motors were prohibited. Nearly all of our earlier years, Jim worked away from home. To me it is quite possible to live that way and still be very family oriented. Every time he went somewhere in the summer, we trailed along if we could.

When construction of the DEW line began, Jim became an assistant superintendent in Barrow. In the summers, the boys and I would join him. We'd drive to Fairbanks, catch a ride on a DC-3 freighter and live in an apartment in half of a

Quonset hut. We ate in the superintendent's mess hall at dinnertime. I also had a little hotplate for lunches. On Sundays Jim would take us out on a small tracked vehicle called a Weasel. We'd take along sandwiches and thermoses of coffee and cocoa and picnic out of the wind in the shelter of the Weasel. One year I hauled our 14-foot aluminum boat and outboard motor in the truck, then shipped it up by plane. On a calm evening when the sun was still shining on the Arctic Ocean, we would join the Eskimo people who were out there in everything from skin boats and oars to much more powerful outboards than we had.

In 1960 I went back to work. I went into the employment office and they hired me on the spot as their secretary. Later I became an interviewer. In 1963 the Manpower Training and Development Act was passed. I asked to be assigned to training and became the assistant to the man in charge of the Anchorage program. In a few months he was sent to Nome and I was left in charge. To my protests that I needed more training, I was told to "read the rules and make judgmental decisions." So I did.

The '64 earthquake was the beginning of a new phase in our life. Jim went to Homer to help rebuild the small boat harbor. He froze his fingers while taking soundings, so could never work again in the Arctic. I was extra busy with retraining courses, as the earthquake had caused such a disruption of regular jobs. Much of that money helped the community college provide the necessary courses. Eventually many of those courses helped UAA grow. A few years later I became the Southcentral area coordinator of ASMUS, a voluntary coalition of African-Americans, Native organizations, local unions and the Department of Labor. The pipeline had been authorized, and Alaskans wanted its citizens to build it. It was hectic, but I feel we were quite successful.

I retired from the Department of Labor in '77 after 17 years. I had learned a lot and thoroughly enjoyed helping others find work. By then both Jim and I had fallen in love with Homer and bought some bay view property in 1967. We built our home there when we retired. We enjoyed fishing and clam-digging and walking the beaches together. We were never society people; we'd just get together with our buddies and visit. Money never meant very much to me, or JP either. We just did the things we liked and had a good time. He died in 1985. I am 85 but I still find a lot of satisfaction and humor, living in Alaska.

Larry "Rocky" Cummins

In 1980 I befriended Rocky Cummins, who was then in his late 80s. A tall, lanky man, he lived on the village airstrip in Talkeetna, just a few doors down from my place.

As a clerk at the B&K (now Nagley's Store), I looked forward to Rocky's visits. He'd arrive at the store on his three-wheeler and spend a considerable amount of time picking out one or two items. I would trail around behind him, full of small talk and big questions. Unlike a lot of the regulars, Rocky never complained about the weather or local politics; he was just happy to be alive. He'd had a nasty run-in with another snowmachiner a couple of years earlier, breaking both his leg and hip.

When his health began to decline, I started visiting Rocky at his home. In that uninhibited setting, he told me of his experiences in World War I and the early days in Alaska. Eventually he allowed me to tape record our conversations, though he never could figure out why anyone would be interested in his stories.

I was born in Illinois and grew up in Canada. I guess I must've got my urge to travel from my uncle, who was the captain of a windjammer. He used to travel the whole world. When he'd come home he'd bring us stuff from all kinds of places. One time he brought home a mummy from South America. We thought that was so great, but our mother told him, "Get that thing out of here!" It turned out it wasn't real, but it sure fooled all of us.

As a young man I did construction work all around the Northwest, building bridges and so forth. In 1912 I went to India, a terrible, hot place, to do some more steel work. I couldn't wait to get back to Canada after that. I was 26 when World War I

started. I happened to be in Winnipeg, so I patriotically joined the cavalry. I soon discovered I wasn't cut out for the cavalry, though, so I came to the U.S., joined the Army and was immediately sent to fight in the trenches of France.

That experience was like nothing you could ever imagine. Think of hell, and then multiply it by about a thousand. If a guy could've seen to shoot, it might've been all right, but there was so much smoke, you couldn't even see the boogers! One thing that really impressed me was this amazing rig, a big boxcar, that held a huge cannon. The Germans could shoot 80 miles away with that thing.

After the war I got my wages - $31.10 - and I went back to Canada. I started logging and doing other stuff, then I drifted up to Alaska, which I'd been told was a place where a feller could get a start.

When I first came here I didn't have a nickel to my name. I made a few dollars fishing, and I did some trapping in the winters. I spent some time in Southeast. That used to be the most beautiful country. The timber had never been cut, and some of those trees were ten feet in diameter.

photo by Roberta Sheldon

Jim Beaver and Rocky Cummins in front of the Fairview Inn, early 60s

The first time I saw Anchorage was in 1926. It was the toughest looking place, all burned off. You could've bought the whole town for $10,000; it was just a bunch of little cabins that no one lived in. If you wanted to, you could just move into one of them.

The town was fairly tame. There was only one policeman and he had nothing to do. The whole time I was there, there was only one murder.

I worked stringing telegraph wire between Anchorage and Seward. The guy I worked with only spoke Finnish. He was determined to teach me his language, but the only thing I ever managed to learn was how to count to ten.

After a while I got the urge to stay in one place, so I built a little tin-roof cabin in the Talkeetna Hills and started gold mining. It was hard rock mining and I never made much money, just enough to get by.

It's nice there on Mount Goldy in the summer, real pretty. There's wildflowers everywhere, they smell so good, and the ground is so spongy, it's just like walking on a thick carpet. I used to have a vegetable garden; they never grew very big but they were tasty, plus I knew where there were lots of blueberries.

I built a water wheel up there. I'd never seen one, but since I didn't have anything better to do, I went to my shop and just kind of fooled around, and by golly the thing worked. I had a blacksmith shop there; it was a portable rig. These days, I don't have any use for tools any more, but I still like to fool around with 'em.

Talkeetna's changed a lot from the old days. There's lots more people, for one thing. In the old days it was just a few miners and trappers. Every now and then they'd get ornery and shoot at one another, but mostly they were real decent people. When I got here there were only four kids in town; they had to wait till there were six to open the school, which was in the Roadhouse.

I had a team of dogs while I was living up on Goldy, and one winter night I heard this big commotion outside. I found my flashlight and, right outside the door, there was a big wolf. He roared at me and I roared right back at him, till he finally went away. Most people don't know that wolves are afraid of humans. They'll jump right on a dog team, though.

One moonlit winter night I got an urge to go to town. The dogs were just starting to run when a wolf came through a birch tree. I'm telling you, those dogs just disappeared. After that I didn't go to town at night unless I had a gun. There used to be a lot of wolves here in Talkeetna; you'd see ten or 20 just across the river. When the moose got thicker they disappeared, but there are still a lot of them up in the mountains.

I guess one of these days I'll end up in the Pioneer Home, though I don't want to. A while back I was in the hospital in Anchorage and there was this old lady, she was 93. The nurses wanted me to go visit her and take her some flowers. I said, "I'm not going over there." But they got hold of me and took me to her room and it turned out I knew her; she was from Copper Center. She was a real nice lady - Spanish - and still real good looking. Unfortunately, her people were coming the next day to take her home. But we got along real good and I asked her to sing me a Spanish

Kitty Banner, Sharon Bushell, Rocky Cummins,
Kathy Sullivan, July 1981

song. I had spent a year in Mexico and I knew a little of the language. She sang for me, and boy was it beautiful.

For decades Rocky's best friend was his airstrip-neighbor, Jim Beaver. The two of them put in plenty of time at the Fairview Inn, bending their elbows and swapping lies. Beaver was younger than Rocky, whom he dubbed "the dinosaur." Their friendship and good-natured antagonism is, to this day, legendary stuff in Talkeetna.

Rocky turned 90 on July 9, 1981. Kitty Banner (one of the original owners of K2 Aviation) baked him a huge chocolate cake, and she and Kathy Sullivan and I took him out for dinner. Afterward the four of us went to the Fairview for a nightcap and, with the help of the townspeople, pulled off a glorious surprise party. Rocky sat at the bar and grinned all night. It was one of those classic events that you wish would never end.

Rocky died in 1983. He now rests near his friend Jim Beaver in the Talkeetna Cemetery.

Helena Bartman Andree

80-year-old Helena Andree is a lifelong Alaskan whose story stretches back to a way of life that no longer exists. Except for a few years spent at a BIA boarding school in the village of Kanakanak, Helena Bartman had lived her whole life in a remote speck of the Bristol Bay region. Her Dutch father landed in Alaska in 1906 and had long been the caretaker of a saltry on the Igushik River, where Helena and her siblings were born and raised. Their Yup'ik mother, a beautiful and skilled seamstress, died during the birth of her fourth child.

My father, William Hugo (Billy) Bartman, was a Dutch adventurer who dreamed of being a sailor. He shipped out of Rotterdam at age 14 as a cabin boy and sailed around the world many times. In 1906 his ship docked in San Francisco and he came upon a group of men talking about Alaska. He had never heard of it before. They told him Alaska was where they went every summer to fish in a wooden sailboat. My dad said, "I wish I could go with you," and one of them said, "Why can't you? Just get your bag. We're leaving in a few days." So that's what he did, he jumped ship and came to Alaska.

The first place they landed was the Nushagak River in Bristol Bay. Dad wanted to winter over, so he went to the superintendent of the Alaska Packers Association Cannery and said he was looking for a job. He ended up staying with them for 40 years.

He was the type of person who was meant for Alaska. He became expert at maneuvering the little Bristol Bay wooden sailing ships and, in the winter, he learned to mush dogs. In 1917 he met his first wife, a native lady, and they had four children.

Then the flu epidemic hit and his wife and two of his children died. When they got to be school age, Dad was required by law to send his surviving daughter and son to a BIA boarding school in Kanakanak.

Not far from there, at the Igushik River, there was a saltry, and the cannery superintendent talked my dad into becoming the caretaker for it. There, with the help of his two sons, Dad raised a nice bunch of dogs, and he got quite friendly with a lot of

Helena Bartman Andree as a teenager

Yup'ik people. He would travel from village to village, hauling mail, freight, passengers, anything he could carry.

In those days it was hard to find someone who was bilingual, but he always traveled with a Native interpreter. On one trip from Dillingham to Togiak, they stopped in Toklong, a little village that no longer exists. There were only 40 or 50 people there, all living in barabara houses. He noticed a lady wearing a beautiful parka and exquisite fur boots and, without knowing a thing about her, he fell madly in love.

The next morning they returned to Toklong. The interpreter talked to the village council, who directed them to the house belonging to the lady's family. Through the interpreter, Dad asked her father if she was available to marry the white man. He said, "We'll have to talk to the rest of the villagers. You come back next month and we'll let you know."

Later on it became almost a status symbol, to have your daughter marry a white man, but in those days it wasn't. The people of the village inquired and found that Dad's reputation was good; he was well liked in all the villages. So it was agreed that Amalia, my mother, could marry him. When Dad returned, he put her in his sled and they went back to Kanakanak, where the commissioner married them. Then they went to the saltry, where I was born and raised, along with my brothers and sisters.

My father was a wonderful man. He appreciated the Native ways; that's why he was so respected. Our mother spoke only Yup'ik to us, but he also wanted us to learn English, so that's what he spoke to us, although by that time he knew quite a bit of Yup'ik.

Mom trapped hundreds of squirrels every summer. She made parkas from the skins and dried the meat. She also dried fish, and taught us all the Native ways of doing things. She did lots of fur work and made all our clothes. She made my father the warmest fur boots, and a canvas-covered sleeping bag of reindeer skin, with the fur inside. My father would frequently get caught in storms, but he was always comfortable in his bag. He hauled freight and passengers by dog team until airplanes came to the country; I think his last trip was 1936.

My mother died in childbirth when I was eight. By then we were old enough that we had to go to school, so we were sent to live at the orphanage in Kanakanak, to attend the boarding school. We didn't want to go; oh my brother cried and cried! Soon thereafter my half-sister from Dad's first marriage died of polio while she was Outside at a BIA school. My dad was so heart-broken, he couldn't bear to send any of his kids away for further education, so I only went through fifth grade.

One of the main turning points of my life came when I was 16. I became deathly sick and there was no way to get me to a hospital. After about a week, Dad snow-shoed to the top of the hill and looked out at Nushagak Bay. He came back all excited; he thought he'd seen the mast of a boat way out there. He and my brothers took the dog sled and, sure enough, there was a boat. He went by kayak to the boat and begged the captain, who agreed to take me to Dillingham.

I was in agony. Just moving my arm sent shock waves through my body. All I could do was try to lay perfectly still. It was 4:00 in the morning when we arrived. The old hospital had burned the year before, so it was a makeshift building, where the BIA staff used to live. They had only two tiny "wards," one for women and one for men.

There was a very nice nurse there, and I have a vivid memory of the old crank telephone she used to call the doctor. He came right over, examined me, and told the nurse that they had to operate right now. They took me into the operating room, which had been the pantry - it was maybe 8' by 10' - put an ether cone over my nose and gave me an appendectomy.

I stayed for six weeks and, during that time, several native women entered the hospital. When I began to feel better, I started interpreting for the doctor. He told me, 'You speak Yup'ik so well, how would you like to be my helper?' I said I'd have to ask my papa, but I was secretly thrilled at the idea. I had done some interpreting earlier, in school. Our teacher was also the magistrate, and one day a dog team came roaring into the schoolyard. This big musher tied up his dogs and in the sled was a small lady. He knocked on the door and, after talking with him, the teacher came to my desk and asked me to interpret.

Here was this pretty Native girl, she was maybe 14, and she acted like she was scared. The teacher said, "This man wants to marry this girl but she doesn't understand English. He wants you to ask her if it's okay." I told her and she started to cry. "No," she said, "I don't want to marry him, but my parents say I should."

In those days, it was the parents who decided, so she married him and away they went. As it turned out, they were a very happy couple. Those types of marriages were still common, and my sister and I were worried that it would happen to us. We were very shy, very timid. We used to hear that maybe men would come and ask Papa if they could marry us, and we were deathly scared of that happening. Whenever men would come to the house, we'd go to our bedroom and stay in there till they left; we didn't even want them to look at us.

After six weeks at the hospital, Dad picked me up in his sailboat and we went home. Finally I told him that I wanted to work in the hospital. He didn't know what to think about that but then he said, "Well you can't go by yourself, you'll have to take your sister." Later he decided he might as well move the whole family, so in September we all went to Dillingham.

My dad, who was known as 'Glass-Eye Billy' Bartman, was an expert sailor. He was able to maneuver his small Bristol Bay sailboat in some of the trickiest waters in Alaska. When it came time to move to Dillingham, he and two friends, along with me, Mary and our ten-year-old brother, Gust, packed the boat with supplies, in preparation for making the 60-mile trip down the Igushik and then up the Nushagak River. Our load was made considerably more cumbersome by the motorboat we were towing for a friend. The second boat held additional household items, plus a makeshift shelter, so that's where Dad put the three of us kids.

When we left our place it was dead calm, our sail was useless, we just drifted with the tide. Dad knew that by the time we got to the mouth of the Nushagak the tide would be coming in and it would take us up river. After a while the sun went down and it got pitch dark. The wind started blowing and it started to rain, hard! There we were, in this rough water, and we could hardly see our dad's boat in front of us. All of a sudden the line holding the motorboat broke and away we went. We were completely out of control, getting farther and farther away. But we didn't know how dangerous it was; we thought it was fun.

I don't know how he did it, but my father was able to circle back around us and, as he came by, he hollered to my brother to get to the bow of the boat, coil his line and throw it when they came by again. Gust tried, but we could hardly even see the other boat. Finally he succeeded, and we tied up again. My poor father was frantic.

Then his mast broke. It came crashing down and went under the boat, so we had no sail. We were just thrashing around, at the mercy of the storm. After a while we ended up on a sandbar, high and dry. That really worried the men. They figured we'd be lucky to live through it. They all fished the Nushagak and they knew we were on the graveyard sands, which had caused the deaths of many fishermen. When the tide came in, it could easily swamp our boats. We dumped all our dry grub, which had gotten wet anyway, to lighten the boat. We huddled around in the fo'c's'le and Dad said, "If anyone knows a prayer, now's the time to say it." Someone must have prayed because just as it started getting light, the wind and rain stopped. When the tide came in, it was dead calm and we floated perfectly.

There was a cannery at Clarks Point, about ten miles from where we were. The men rigged half a mast and we were able to make it there. The caretaker was Henry Shade. He came down to the dock and said, "You were out in that storm?" He couldn't get over how lucky we were. He rigged us up with a new mast and we continued our journey.

At that time Kanakanak village consisted of about seven families, plus the BIA hospital crew. I worked as a patient interpreter at the hospital and Mary worked as a helper in the laundry. The doctor used to brag about what a good interpreter I was, to the local storekeepers. The manager of one of them told me he did a lot of Native business and he offered me a job. That really appealed to me because I wanted to be around more Native people. I loved speaking Yup'ik.

I lacked confidence with the English language and, because I didn't speak it fluently; it sounded broken to me. But the Native language was so beautiful. As children we were all very proud that we could speak it so easily. The elders always told us, "Don't ever lose that."

So I became a clerk at Lowe's Store and I loved it. I worked there 24 years. I'd be there still if it hadn't burned down. When I first started working there, hardly a Native spoke English, so I was always asked to interpret. There was a bench in the store where the villagers would sit and visit. I used to leave my work and go jabber with them. At that time a lot of people were moving in, the area was growing.

One of my co-workers was a very kind and helpful man, Bill Roberts. He and I went together for two years and married in 1941. Bill died seven years later of TB, at home. It's a wonder the rest of us didn't get it; TB was everywhere in those days and we didn't really take any precautions. We had four children and, when I later married Al Andree, we had one more child. Al and I were married for 42 years.

After Lowe's burned in 1960, I worked as a bilingual dispatcher for Western Alaska Airlines, which I thoroughly enjoyed. Ten years later I found a job I liked even better. In the early 70's, as people started looking at the alcohol problem among Natives, helping my people became my biggest goal, so I trained to be an alcohol and drug counselor.

Previously there had been so much shame about alcoholism, but now people were looking at it as a disease, something that could be dealt with. There were only seven of us Native counselors originally, and we were very fortunate to get the most extensive training you can imagine. We went to Indian reservations Outside, exchanging ideas and learning all kinds of new things. Then we traveled all over Alaska, sharing what we had learned. We held training sessions for social workers, counselors, school teachers and public health employees. For a while it looked like we were making some real inroads, but it's such a huge problem, and eventually a lot of the money dried up. I kept my office open in Dillingham on a volunteer basis. Now, 20 years later, I still belong to an elder group that's actively working on the problem. We make presentations to various groups, always focusing on how important it is for parents to take more of a role in educating their young ones.

I loved living in Dillingham, but while I was working for the airlines, I started coming down to Homer on a regular basis, to visit my daughter, Audrey. Eventually I fell in love with the area, so I told Al, "You'd better come and take a look." He loved it too. He was always one for beaches and water, so we moved here in 1980. I feel so blessed. I have four wonderful children, lots of grandchildren and many great-grandchildren.

Lyle West

I was born in 1916 in a little town near Sioux Falls, South Dakota. I lived through the dust bowl and a lot of hard times. My dad was a dry land horse farmer. I can remember coming in at noon to eat dinner and having to light the flat wick lamp, it was that dark from the dust. It would drift so much, it'd drift the fences under. I agree with an old guy from Kansas who once told me, "You can be born and raised somewhere, and there's nothing you can do about that. But if you spend the rest of your life there, that's your own damn fault."

Farming was too risky for me. I quit high school in my sophomore year and went to work in a garage for ten dollars a week. I mechaniced in the winter and carpentered in the summer. Then the war came along and there was suddenly all kinds of work. I'd been wanting to come to Alaska for a long time. In 1943 I was working in Cheyenne and I saw an ad in the Denver paper, saying they needed construction workers in Alaska. They'd pay your way up here and back if you stayed a year. So here I come.

They sent me to work on the Canol pipeline, which most people have never heard of. It was a three-inch line from Skagway to Whitehorse and then on to Fairbanks, for the purpose of getting fuel up there for the lend-lease planes we were sending to Russia. After that I helped build a pump station at 33 mile on the Richardson Highway. When that job was over, they sent me back to South Dakota. I was glad of that. I had three kids there and a little money saved up, so I went back and finished up the house.

In November of '44 they needed workers in the Aleutians, so I signed up. They put

700 of us in a liberty boat, with bunks so close together, you couldn't raise your knees up or you'd bump the guy above you. There was a big storm in the Pacific. I didn't know I could get that sick and still live. I swear I got blisters on my back from sliding back and forth in that canvas bunk. Everybody cusses the Aleutians, but not me. I was so glad to get off that boat. We landed at Adak and later they sent me out to Shemya.

When the war ended I came back home. All during the war nobody could get any parts or equipment. Their cars and trucks and tractors were worn out, so they started beating a path to my door, to fix their stuff. I thought, if there's that much work I'll build a shop, I don't want to work out under a tree all winter.

Just about the time I got my shop finished, the OPA (Office of Price Administration) jumped in and put some severe restrictions on what I could charge. So I ended up opening at $1.25 an hour shop time, and hell, the farm hands were getting a dollar an hour.

Lyle West in 1950, proud owner of a Cessna 140

For a year and a half I about worked myself to death. I had a waiting list when I opened the shop and I never did get caught up. Then I saw another ad in the paper, they needed construction workers up north again. I got to Fairbanks in July of '47 and I've been in Alaska ever since.

I worked at Eielson Air Force Base for 17 months, getting it ready for the B-36s that were coming up. We spent the winter in a tent with an oil stove in the middle. Fortunately that wasn't a cold winter; the worst it got was about 40 below. They had the tent walls framed up with ship lap outside and Celotex on the inside. You could cut a little hole in the Celotex alongside your bed and keep your ice cream in there, and it wouldn't melt. We also had a ship lap floor. You got to where you'd take your shoes off at night and set 'em up on a box or a chair, 'cause if you set 'em on the floor, they'd freeze there and in the morning you'd have to kick 'em loose. Over the years I worked on many of the buildings at UAF (University of Alaska at Fairbanks). I built the president's house in '53 and '54. When construction got slow, I took over the maintenance crew for three years. Eventually I went back to construction.

I lived and worked in Fairbanks for a long time, and it took me 15 years to get in the mood to homestead. I filed on 160 acres in Goldstream Valley in '58, but I didn't get all my cultivation requirements done in time, and I wound up with 80 acres. I had a little 12' by 16' shack on the edge of town, I loaded that up and moved it out to the homestead and built a lean-to on it. Then I started working on a better house.

Several of us went together and bought a sawmill. I sat in my little shanty all winter, drawing plans for my house. The shanty kept getting smaller and my plans kept getting bigger, and I wound up with an 1800 square foot place. It took me 20 years to get it done, building out of pocket and in my spare time.

When I first moved onto the homestead, I hadn't had a chance to get my winter firewood.There were lots of times I'd be on the job all day, then after work I'd have to get wood. I'd drive my old Model A Ford as far as I could, stop and put on the chains, then plow through the snow until I found a dead tree to cut down. I'd haul it back, cut it up, and then I could get myself some supper.

The road wasn't any too good in those early days, and lots of times it was easier to walk it than to fight it. I often walked five miles in the morning, went to work, then walked back in. Eventually I had three old rigs. In the spring when the road got bad, I'd drive one of 'em till it got stuck in a mud hole, then I'd get my Cat and pull it out. I'd transfer to another of my rigs, drive as far as I could - a mile or so - then get in the other one.

In '83 I sold my homestead and moved to Homer. I'd met an old Norwegian oiler back in '43 and he described Homer like it was a paradise, so I'd always wanted to see it. I moved down here and built myself a shop and a house. Those were both one-man projects. I'm used to doing things by myself.

I don't spend much time in the house, I'm usually out in my shop. Not too long ago I made four grandfather clocks for my kids and grandkids. I'd already made one, so I thought, I'll make four of 'em all at the same time; it won't take much longer than making just one. Well that's true in one way, but I was awful glad when I got that fourth one done, I can tell you that. It took me several months.

Besides work and music, traveling is what I like to do. I go Outside and ramble quite a bit, see all those places I've read about, take some pictures. I always was a big fan of old country music and bluegrass. I had a friend who worked on Eielson, he was a good, old-time fiddler from North Carolina. He retired in the late 60s, and moved back home. I started going down there on a regular basis to visit him. We'd go to bluegrass festivals, three or four day events, and the sound guys would always let me patch right into their boards. As a result, I've got a whole lot of music tapes.

Since I was a kid, flying was something I always wanted to do. I started taking lessons at Weeks Field in Fairbanks. I soloed after four hours and 20 minutes, then got my ticket (license) Outside, in 1950. I bought a Cessna 140, a little tail dragger, and flew it back up with just 40 hours solo. My buddy and I used to fly to Chena Hot springs for a bath; it only took two dollars worth of gas to fly there and back. The hot springs was quite a place in the old days. Miners would go up there and soak their aches and pains in that mineral water all winter.

I've always liked working. One day this last June I was out puttering around my shop. I got pretty busy, I worked about 13 hours, and it wasn't till I looked at the paper that night that I realized it was my 85th birthday. I had a buddy from Oklahoma while I was working in Fairbanks. He had some pretty good old Okie expressions. One of 'em was, "It's surprising what a feller can do when he don't know when to quit." I guess that's about how it is with me.

Emely DuBeau

Emely Abrahamson, born and raised in Seattle, traded in big city life for four years of almost total isolation in Alaska. In 1937 she, her husband, and their young son moved to Herendeen Bay, halfway down the Alaska Peninsula. Their nearest neighbors were 35 miles away. They received mail and supplies twice a year and socialized almost as infrequently. Emely, who became known up and down the Peninsula as "Blondie," tells her story with good humor, but assures me: She would never choose to repeat it.

For several years during the early 1930s, my two teenage brothers, Hank and Alvin, fished on sailboats in Bristol Bay. One year their ship wrecked outside of Nelson Lagoon, on the Bering Sea. The villagers took them in, let them stay the winter, and treated them very well. After that my brothers always told me, "There's no place like Alaska. You'd better come up here."

A few years later I was married to Fran "Frenchie" DuBeau, and we had a year-old son, Pete. My brothers told Frenchie endless stories, that in Alaska all you had to do was step outside your cabin, shoot a caribou, and you'd have all the meat you could eat. The same thing with catching fish. Frenchie liked the sounds of that, so in October, 1937 the three of us packed up and came to Alaska. We took the Alaska steamship, stayed one night in Seward, then took the steamer *Star* to Sand Point. By that time we had been aboard ship for two weeks, and I was seasick the whole way.

My brother Hank came from the other side of the Alaska Peninsula, which was a nine-mile portage, to meet us. We then took a little skiff to a place called Dead Man's Cove, on the Pacific side. We spent a night in an old trapper's shack, and the next day walked the nine miles, which was all hills and dales and creeks. Hank was packing my son, and whenever we'd cross a creek, Pete's feet would dangle in the water.

Coming from the Northwest, that Aleutian country was completely foreign to me. There were no trees, just alders and willows, and the wind blew relentlessly. We stayed the first winter with Hank and his trapping partner, an old man named Otto Skoog. Otto was a real character, a big jolly man with a huge beard. He looked just like Santa Claus.

Emely DuBeau and her son, Pete

We'd only been there about four weeks when I developed a bad toothache. The three men decided they'd better pull the tooth, so Hank skied across the bay to a cannery. He knew the watchman there had some forceps. Otto sat me down and gave me a big glass of rum and an orange. He said, "Take a swallow of this and then suck on that orange, and I promise, when you finish the glass, you won't feel a thing."

He was right. At the last minute Hank took the forceps from Frenchie, claiming he was stronger and could do a better job. Instead of pulling the tooth, though, he squeezed it and broke it right down to the bone. The next morning I had the worst hangover, and it was four more years until I was able to get my tooth repaired.

The men trapped in the winter and fished in the summer, which was really delightful for them; they only worked a few months out of the year. But a woman's life was all work, morning, noon and night. It seems like I was always hauling water, chopping

Frenchie DuBeau in Herendeen Bay, 1938

wood, or washing clothes. I cooked on a tiny wood stove. I did a lot of canning: berries, fish, caribou, ducks, geese.

I only saw one woman that first year. In the middle of the winter, an old Eskimo lady named Emma came to visit me. She was from the Diomede Islands, and I thoroughly enjoyed her company; she was very sweet. But she had tribal marks on her face and two great big teeth that looked like fangs, and poor little Pete was scared to death. Our second year, we moved into a little one-room cabin, right on a creek. I'll always remember our first Thanksgiving dinner there: porcupine, stuffed and cooked just like turkey. It was delicious.

We papered the inside of the cabin with old magazines we found when we moved in. I had always been a voracious reader but I hadn't thought to bring any books when we left Seattle. I'd start reading a story from one of the magazines and then have to go around the whole house, looking for the next page.

I had a treadle sewing machine, so I made Pete's clothes, even his snow suits. I knitted socks, caps and mittens for all of us too. We had to send to Sears for the rest of our clothing. We didn't send them money in exchange for our goods; we always sent furs. Frenchie was a real good trapper.

The nearest neighbors, where there might be a woman and children, was 35 miles away, at Port Moller. We kept in contact with the other people at Herendeen Bay by Morse Code. The men put together a key with a coil and battery and we talked by dit-dit-dit-dit at a set time, every day. It was picked up by our radios so we knew who was sick and peoples' day to day activities.

We only got groceries twice a year, in the spring and fall, when the cannery boats came in to Port Moller. That was really the only time we ever saw the people who lived around there. It was a pretty isolated existence. There was only one other white woman in the area. Occasionally we had visitors. Whenever we saw a boat approach, we knew we'd have company for a week or two. Usually they were storm-bound, so we'd make beds all over the floor and add more beans to the pot.

Each May we used to go to a place called Gull Island and pick seagull eggs. We'd get a big barrel and put about a thousand eggs into it, with a certain preservative, and they would last the whole winter. The eggs had a strong taste; I didn't care for them, but Frenchie and Pete thought they were fine. I used them a lot for cooking.

On one occasion I had to be a midwife. My sister-in-law's baby was coming, and the regular midwife couldn't get there because of a storm. Fortunately for both of us, when I was 15, I'd seen my sister being born, plus I'd had a child myself. My sister-in-law was in labor for 30 hours and we were all getting pretty worried. I didn't know what to do, but the child was born just fine.

Though I had no medical training, I had to deal with other emergency situations. There was a little Native boy with an abscess behind his ear; his mother sent some kids by dog team to get me. He had lost a lot of weight and he couldn't eat, so we got in contact by radio with the doctor in Unalaska and he talked us through the procedure of lancing the abscess and draining it.

We left Herendeen Bay when Pete was five. It was time for him to go to school, plus he needed playmates. We went to Seward, and that's where we stayed for the next 40 years. Frenchie worked as a longshoreman and a carpenter. He was well known in Seward because he was always full of gab. We had good friends in Seward, but most of them have moved away or died. When Frenchie got sick, we moved to Anchorage and I've been here ever since. Whenever I go Outside, which isn't very often, I can't be gone more than just a few days. As soon as I get where I'm going, I start thinking, *what in the world am I doing here*, and I can't wait to get back. There's a certain freedom in Alaska that you don't find Outside. I don't know what it is; I can't pinpoint it. I just know I feel freer up here.

Chuck Porter

I was born in Port Orchard, Washington in 1922. When I was ten my parents divorced and my mom and I moved to Craig, Alaska, where she married Ellis Reynolds. Ellis was the postmaster and also a bookkeeper for a guy named Bill Rushbaugh, a great old German entrepreneur. He had a grocery store, which Ellis ran. Mom worked at Jim Lusher's clothing store.

Craig had a population of about four or five hundred in those days. There were a couple hundred Indian kids and only three white kids and we all got along fine. There were no vehicles and no roads in Craig. They had a walkway of two 2 by 12s spaced apart, so that hand trucks could move stuff around the town.

When I was 12 I went to work for Bill Ricewine as a deckhand on his boat. Later, at about 13, I was helping buy fish. Around that same time I got my own skiff, a 14-footer, which I had found the bare bones of on the beach. I befriended an old boat maker and helped him "clinker-build" the hull with overlapping pieces of wood. We clinched 'em together with copper nails. We did it in our spare time and it was a fine skiff. I had a little five-horse Johnson outboard motor for it. I used to go over to Crab Bay, spear Dungeness crab, cook them, and sell them for 50 cents a piece.

In about 1937 I went to live with my father and stepmother in Fairbanks. While I was there I got a summer job prospecting for a gold mining company, the F.E. Company. This old guy named Charlie and I were flown out to a place called the Bonnefield gold district in an old Stinson. We landed on top of a mountain and had to pack all our stuff down to an old abandoned cabin about three miles away.

We fixed the cabin up and used it for home base. Old Charlie, he had all the trappings. He had a five-gallon can made into an oven so we could put it on top of a stove and make bread and biscuits and pancakes. He brought some sourdough starter. He knew what to do.

We kept busy. We went back up on top of the mountain and filled in all the drainage ditches so that we could be resupplied every now and then. I learned how to gold pan. I also built a pond, put some grayling in it, and after that we had fresh trout whenever we wanted them.

The mosquitoes were so thick, I had to wear a head net. I'd look back at Charlie and there wouldn't be a single mosquito on him anywhere; I always used to marvel at that. He'd tell me, "Ah they just love young blood. They never come after me."

Chuck Porter in Craig, 1936

When I came home, I got a job in the Piggly Wiggly butcher shop, right next door to where we lived. I had worked all summer, then at the butcher shop, so when my dad told me I couldn't go to the junior prom, I gathered up my money and belongings and took off. I found one of the truckers I was friends with and he agreed to drive me to Valdez. When I got there I bought a ticket on an Alaska steamship for Juneau under an assumed name in steerage. I was 16. When I got to Juneau, there was Ellis standing on the dock. It all turned out okay; they were all very relieved to see me, which I hadn't expected. So there I was, back in Juneau again, and glad of it.

After school I worked for my Uncle Percy at his restaurant, making ice cream in the basement. Percy's was the place to go to meet up with your friends before, during and after school. I also delivered papers. My route was from Main Street down to the rock dump. Another of my jobs was setting up the pins at the bowling alley. The kids I met at Juneau High are still some of the closest friends I've ever had. I wasn't a great student, but I did study French, which came in very handy while I was in Europe during World War II. My worst subject was English. Thank goodness for Gloria White, the girl who sat in front of me.

After graduation I went out to a place called Deer Harbor on the outer coast, near Sitka, to buy fish with another young guy. We worked all summer. When the time came to move the barge back to winter quarters, a guy by the name of Kinky Beers came out with a boat to tow us in. After we had passed out of the entrance, the swells got pretty good size. When we got about 300 yards out into the ocean, the tow line broke. There was nothing we could do, so we grabbed our rifles and sleeping bags and the money, then managed to get the side door open on the lee side of the scow. We were drifting up on the rocks pretty fast. We had a flat-bottom skiff on board, which we dumped into the water. We jumped into that and paddled into the harbor. Meanwhile Kinky had taken the boat and run it into the harbor also, so all was well on that score.

The next day we went out and the scow had drifted up on top of a great big flat rock, so between the crew of the boat and the other kid and myself, we salvaged as much of the groceries and gear as we could, down over the rock piles and into the big boat. We didn't take the trolling leads; they were just too heavy. Ultimately we got back to Juneau and, because we hadn't gotten the leads out, the people at the cold storage were going to withhold some of my wages, which was about $500, a pretty good chunk of money in those days. But ultimately calm heads prevailed and I got my money.

After graduation I decided it was time for me to go south. I was thinking of going to a junior college in Los Angeles, and the day I left just so happened to be December 7th, 1941. We were at Marlene Island, about seven miles south of Juneau, when we heard the news about the bombing of Pearl Harbor. The boat traveled blacked out the rest of the way to Seattle.

In Los Angeles I applied for the Air Force cadet program; I wanted to be a pilot. Ultimately I got Orville Osborn, a friend of mine from Juneau, to come to LA, and he got into the cadet program too. We started our training at Camp Hahn, then they shipped us out to Barstow, in the desert, where it got up to a hundred-something during the day. Kids from Alaska don't take too well to such hot weather. To get out of there, we volunteered for KP duty back at Camp Hahn. I finished my training as bombardier/navigator and was made an instructor, then sent overseas. All in all I had 42 missions over enemy-held territory.

While I was in California, I married a girl I had gone to high school with. When I returned to Juneau, she and our two children met me there and life returned to normal. I got my dispatcher's license and became a meteorologist and navigation instructor, as well as a dispatcher.

I got a job at Pacific Northern Airlines and did a variety of jobs: ticket issuer, baggage manager and whatever else needed doing. I used to radio the pilots regarding the weather they'd be encountering. Eventually I made up the weather pattern for the whole Gulf of Alaska each day. I was with PNA in Juneau from 1947 until 1957, then I transferred to Anchorage and worked for them until 1967.

In 1967 my second wife, Annie, and I moved back to Juneau and I took a job as part owner and manager of Concrete Sand and Gravel. I worked full time for them until '87, and in '91 I retired. Annie and I now live in a condo on the shoreline of Douglas, overlooking Juneau. As I'm recording this, a whale just went by the house; he's headed up for the flats. We also have eagles and ducks, mostly mallards, that come by. They've found a haven in front of our place. No one shoots them along this beach, so they come and feed and stay all winter long.

Although I'm coming to the end of my life, overall I feel I've been very lucky. Lucky to have done the many things I've done, and lucky that I was able to spend most of my life in Alaska.

Frances Ray

I grew up in Dillon, Montana. My mother immigrated to the United States from Czechoslovakia when she was 19, married my gold miner father at 20, and immediately had five children. When she was 28, Dad was killed in a snow slide, so she had a difficult life for quite a while. She'd had no education, so she cleaned houses in order to make a little money. Eventually she remarried and things got better. She lived to be 91.

Maybe because Mother was unable to have an education, it meant so much to her that her children did. She was thrilled when I graduated from college. I taught business classes in high school for a couple of years, then World War II came along.

I had long been fascinated by Alaska, though I can't say when or why that began. As the war began to escalate, everyone wanted to do their part. I was single and looking for some adventure, so I tried to get into the Navy. They wouldn't take me, though, because of my eyesight. So in July of '44 I signed a one-year contract with the Civil Service, to work in ordnance supply for the Air Force in Anchorage. They paid my way up, and when my year was up, they would pay my way back.

I'll never forget my first impression of Anchorage: What a dump! 4th Avenue had very little pavement. The base was all camouflaged and it was so dreary. Even the Chugach Mountains, which I have come to love, seemed dreary to me.

But there were things about Alaska that I liked right away. There were lots of interesting young people and, because we had arrived in summer, the nonstop daylight was enchanting. We lived on base and each morning a bus would come and

Frances and Bill Ray, Fort Richardson 1945

take us to work.

Pretty soon there was quite a crowd of us who became good friends. There was a popular nightclub called the Lido that we used to frequent, and we'd often stop at the South Seas, where Wally Hickel tended bar.

It's funny, because we women used to get teased all the time, that we'd come to Alaska to find husbands. Speaking strictly for myself, I can say that was definitely not the case. But before very long I did meet a most wonderful man, William C. Ray, and after that my impression of Alaska jumped another big notch. Bill was a man who loved to have fun, and he made a tourist of me, because he also loved to drive. There weren't many roads in those days, and they were all gravel, but we drove every one of them, many times. We drove to Copper Center, to Eureka, to Petersville. We went to Palmer with friends every Sunday for dinner; I wish I could think of the name of that place; they had the most marvelous pie. We drove to Fairbanks on the Tok Highway. We drove the Alaska Highway in '47 and several times after that.

After we married in 1945, we lived in the married couples quarters on the base, then I got a job teaching school downtown, so we had to move off the base. Housing in those days was very scarce, and you pretty much took anything you could get. We ended up moving into a funny little place on 5th and Gambell that was really just one big room with a bed and a tiny kitchen. There was an outhouse in the alley and the boards didn't quite match, so when you were sitting out there, you could watch the traffic go by. It sounds funny now but, believe me, it wasn't funny then.

Fortunately, we had friends who were living in a nice apartment where the

Westmark is now. There was a vacancy and we were able to get it. It was small but, to us, it was incredibly luxurious. And it was only a block from where I worked, at the Anchorage High School. All 12 grades were in the two buildings where the PAC is now.

We moved to Petersburg for three years, then returned to Anchorage in 1950. Bill got a job on the White Alice project, but I couldn't get back in the school system right away, so I went to work for NBA (National Bank of Alaska). Housing was still scarce, so they offered us an apartment, which was really just a little house on 3rd Avenue that had been divided into tiny apartments. We lived there until we found a little house out in Spenard. Imagine ... a small unfinished, two-bedroom house on a creek, with two lots, all for $4000. Over time we bought the lots all around us and ended up with an acre and a quarter. We finished the little house, then built a much bigger one. We loved that place. I lived 50 years in that location.

In 1953, when the city started planning the community college, they hired me to work in the office. When the school opened its doors in February of 1954, it was considered part of Anchorage High, which by that time had moved to its current location on Romig Hill. I worked in the office and also taught a couple of classes, then in 1957 I went back to full-time teaching at Anchorage High (it didn't become West High until about 1961).

I really think that teaching then was a whole lot easier than it is now. Students were more cooperative. Parents were more cooperative. Teachers had more authority. I think about all the terrible, violent things that happen in schools today and it seems a little absurd, that back in the old days we worried about students whispering and chewing gum. In the 1940s there wasn't even a dress code; it was just taken for granted that students would wear proper attire. Dress codes didn't come along until the late '50s and '60s

I'll always remember my first big trip, to Japan in 1966, accompanying my husband on business. In those days there were rules of propriety, and if you were a certain age, you just went along with them. I wore a hat, high-heeled shoes, and a coat with a fur collar. I wore those high heels every where I went. Now that I travel a lot, I wouldn't think of wearing anything but my Reeboks and a leisure suit.

I'll always be glad that I went into teaching. It was a good fit for me. I worked with some really excellent people, and I was one of those nutty types who really enjoys being around high school students. From time to time I run into former students, and it's always gratifying, to see familiar faces and occasionally even receive a compliment. Both Bill and I both retired in 1976. We had 20 wonderful years of traveling and playing, doing whatever we wanted, then he died in 1994.

I volunteer at the museum and the visitor's bureau and, once in a while, at the concert association. I still travel a lot. I'll be in Nome for the finish of the Iditarod, and I just got back from a trip to the Amazon. I go with friends to the Performing Arts Center a lot, and every month a group of us go to Cyrano's. I've always loved to bicycle and, now that I've turned 80, I've outfitted my bike with an electric motor, in case I need a little help.

There's still plenty to do and much to be thankful for.

Minnie Swanda

Talkeetna old-timer, Minnie Swanda, died at the age of 92 on January 9, 2001. Minnie and I became well acquainted 20-some years ago, when I rented a cabin from her. She had long been the cook at the Talkeetna Elementary School, and would remain at her post another ten years, retiring in 1991.

Minnie would often visit me at the B & K, where I worked behind the counter. She was in her early 70s then, with mounds of snowy white hair and a devilish temperament. I was a captive audience for her deadpan humor. Every few days she'd stop in and share with me her opinions about the country, the state and the village.

Drinking store coffee and sneaking puffs off a cigarette (she was supposed to have quit), she'd occasionally get contemplative and turn her attention toward the Susitna River. That's when the stories would come rolling out, about the early days in Alaska. About how difficult it had been to leave her parents and siblings for a place so far away.

Part of FDR's New Deal in 1935 was to transplant 200 economically troubled families from the Midwest to Alaska, where they would homestead the Matanuska Valley. Frank Swanda had heard of the program, and it interested him. His wife Minnie didn't share his enthusiasm.

We heard all the ballyhoo about it on the radio, but I didn't pay any attention. When Frank finally convinced me he was serious, right away I began thinking of all the reasons I couldn't leave Minnesota. I'd always been real close to my parents As the oldest of six children, I'd helped my mother raise the family. When we married, Frank and I moved into the house next door. In 1935 I was 27, with two

children of my own.

We really had no idea what we were getting into. Alaska was so far away. The only thing we'd ever learned about it in school was that it was full of ice and snow. We had exactly ten days to sort through all our belongings and say goodbye to our families and friends.

Each of the colonist families was allowed 2,000 pounds of personal belongings. Our family, which included six-year-old Dorothy and two-month-old Butch (Frank Jr.), boarded the train in Pine City and arrived in St. Paul two hours later. I wore

Minnie Swanda in the late 30s

boots and knickers and a leather jacket with a fringe, which shocked everyone. I wasn't about to dress up, though. I knew what a long train ride was like, and besides, I was a pioneer.

Four days later we rolled into San Francisco. I think a lot of those San Francisco people must have thought we were all a bunch of hillbillies. Everyone was out to show us a good time, which was nice and all that. But it was unnerving, like they thought we were going off to the end of the earth and they were the last people who had a chance to be nice to us.

Six days and many bouts of seasickness later, the ship arrived in Seward, but most everyone was quarantined for three days due to an outbreak of measles among the children. We finally reached Palmer on May 10th. There we found a frenzy of activity. Hundreds of CCC (Civilian Conservation Corps) workers were busily putting up tents. Lumber was being moved and stacked. Bags and boxes were being shuffled from the train. There were lots of reporters and photographers, snapping photos and asking questions.

There were very few tents set up when we arrived. There was mud up to our knees, the wind was blowing and it was colder than Billy B. Damned. I was carrying the baby and Frank carried Dorothy. A few tents were up, but there was nothing in them, and they weren't fastened down. There was supposed to be a commissary stocked with food, but all it was was a little store with almost nothing in it. I was mad. Frank was furious.

We were able to locate some of our belongings - the mattress, baby buggy and one barrel of food. We moved our stove into one of the tents and got it set up. Early the next

Minnie and Frank Swanda

morning I got up and made three loaves of bread. The smell of that bread baking, I swear I've never smelled anything so good.

The next day was May 23, the day of the lottery that would determine the location of each family's farm. Our original draw was way the hell and gone, almost all the way to Wasilla. Fortunately, you could trade with whoever was willing. So we ended up with land that friends of our had drawn, south of town, about half a mile from where the Pioneer Home is.

We lived in the tent city until mid-December. Frank herded horses, then started putting up chimneys. I fished and picked berries, and of course, there were the kids to watch. There was an epidemic of German measles that summer, which both my kids got. Our children eventually recovered, but other children in the colony died.

The neighbors helped each other build their homes. Our land had already been cleared and readied for planting, which put us ahead of some of the others. We moved into our place five days before Christmas.

Dorothy was in school then, which was held in one of the railroad cars. I had cows to milk, 75 chickens and two hogs to tend. But I was raised on a farm, and to me all that hard work was just the way life was. We took in seven men, workers from the CCC, who boarded in our home. I was busy, cooking all the time.

I look back on it now, and I remember how my heart just sank when Frank told me he wanted to join the colonists. All I wanted to do was stay in Minnesota. But you know how it is ... you live here a few years and then .... there's just no place quite like Alaska.

For the majority of her life, cooking remained Minnie's mainstay. When the Swandas left Palmer they moved to Anchorage where, for 20 years, they owned and operated the Black and White Cafe, and later the Garmin Hotel. In 1961 Frank and Minnie moved to Talkeetna. Frank ran a guide service there until his death in 1970.

In addition to her job at the elementary school, Minnie helped start the Talkeetna Historical Museum and was active in nearly every organization in town: the VFW, Mat-Su Seniors, and Business and Professional Women, Talkeetna Fire Department Emblem Club, the Catholic Church. At age 80 she proudly received her GED.

John Ireland

87-year-old John Ireland considers his many years as a hermit in the Talkeetna Mountains the best part of his life. For 22 years he lived alone in a small cabin at Murder Lake, where he became an active participant in nature's ongoing drama.

After World War II was over and I got out of the service, I spent a few years in central Oregon. It seemed a little too confining, though. I was a young fellow and I needed some space to wander around in. I finally made the jump and came to Anchorage in 1951, where I ran a second hand furniture store in Mountain View. Alaska was a territory in those days and you could do just about anything. If it suited you, when you were driving along the road and you saw a moose, and if it was moose season or close to it, you could stop your car and go hunt the moose. We used to call that road hunting.

Fifteen years in Anchorage was plenty for me. In 1966 I got pretty disgusted with the antics of humanity and tried to find a more congenial lifestyle alone in the wilderness. I had a friend who lived up in the Talkeetna Mountains, at Stephan Lake. It was all BLM land in those days, and half a mile away there was a smaller lake. I looked the area over and it suited me pretty well, so I put in a homesite claim for five acres. I built a little cabin, using all dead spruce that I found within a quarter-mile of my camp site.

There was plenty to keep me occupied. I fished, hunted, gardened and spent a lot of time tooling leather goods, which I sold wholesale to various places. When I felt like being social, or needed to earn some money, I did a little guiding. Between guiding and leather work, I was able to make my living expenses.

John Ireland inside his well-stocked cabin

In those days the price of groceries and flights was a lot less than today. I was living on $600 or $700 dollars a year. That bought everything: food, trips to town, hotels, rental vehicles, the whole works. I tell people, "It's like the Vermont farmer who says he doesn't live on income, he lives on lack of expense." It was unbelievably economical living.

At first I came to town about every three months. As I got better at shopping and the prices of flying went up, I only came in once in the summer and once in the winter. I got pretty efficient. I would rent a truck and complete my six months shopping in three and a half days. By then I'd be more than ready to go home. I didn't like to leave the place for very long, especially in the wintertime. Something could happen to the weather; there could be a lot of overflow on the lake. You could get stuck out for a couple of weeks.

One thing I loved doing at the lake was listening to the radio. I rigged up a wonderful system, with two radios close together. The battery power was on one and the other one was hooked to the outdoor antenna. There was a field around the outdoor antenna that the other one picked up, and I got the most wonderful reception. Plus there was no static, and when you're out in a remote place, static can be a real plague. I got KGO in San Francisco. I'd get stations from Siberia. I'll never forget, one station's theme song was from Tchaikovsky's "Little Russian Suite." I loved that tune.

To me it was an ideal way to live. I went into the woods expecting to be alone, but after a while the wild creatures began to accept me, and I developed my own culture with them. Soon I began to feel absorbed into the wilderness. Certain birds became unbelievably tame; the gray jays and the boreal, brown-headed chickadees would come to be fed every day. I trained the jays to land on my hand. I'd hold out meat trimmings and each bird in his turn, according to the pecking order, would land on my fingers, take his piece and go. Then the next one would come. When I got tired of holding that greasy meat in my hand, I started putting it on a tin can. They'd come and land on the edge of it and get their own piece of meat. Over the years I had lots of fun with the birds.

There was a yearling bull moose, he got so tame he practically followed me around. There were certain other creatures that I got very close with, a sea gull, a marten and a beaver, to name just a few.

I decided to undertake the writing of a book, to share my experiences, the idea being that I might act as a voice for the environment and its creatures. I worked on the book for several years, and got a printer from a Southeastern community to make 300 copies. The printer was to get his money back before I got any, but he priced the book too low, so I've gotten very little money from it. When all 300 copies sold out, I contacted him about making more, and was told that he had moved to a place in Nevada. Apparently, along the way, his printing press fell off his truck and broke. The last I heard from him he was dickering for parts. But he's from the foot-dragging fraternity, and I don't think I'll see any more copies of it published in my life time. So I tell people, "It's become a rare book already."

When I got to be about 75 I thought I'd better return to civilization. I began to find that I wasn't learning so much anymore, and when the learning stopped it became less interesting. I also wanted to get my book published. Plus, the winter work was becoming difficult for me.

When I left the woods I didn't think I'd like it, and I was correct. I went looking for a place to live; I even went Outside. Michigan was one of the better places. Then I looked at Homer, which is a small community at the edge of a bluff. It was sort of wild, and I figured that if town got too much for me, I could just walk out of it. I had one friend there, and he invited me to

John Ireland fishing at Murder Lake

stay with him while I eased my way back into civilization.

I've been working with leather for 61 years, so if I'm not mistaken, I'm probably the most experienced leather worker in Alaska. Over the years I've had various students. My current student does most of the work now. My vision has gotten quite poor and I tire quickly.

What's the most important thing I learned from living in the woods? Never take anything for granted. You can never tell what's going to happen, so you don't make assumptions. Constantly investigate your surroundings. Make sure about everything.

Betty Epps Arnett

Betty Epps grew up in Knoxville, Tennessee. Her family had strong Methodist ties, and she set her sites on a church-related career. In her teen years she decided on a specific goal: to teach school in a Methodist children's home.

In those days you really had to have a good reason to go to college, if you were female and you were in the south. My father had the opinion that girls didn't need to go to college, but my brother helped me persuade him that my goal was worthy. I got my degree in education from the University of Tennessee and was encouraged to apply for a short-term mission program. It was sort of a forerunner of the Peace Corps, with young people making a two or three-year commitment.

I was given the choice of going to either Alaska or Japan, so I chose Alaska. I got six weeks of training, but nothing, really, that was useful. For what I was about to do, I needed to learn how to be a mother, a referee, a nurse, and a psychologist, all rolled into one. I hadn't even done any babysitting.

In the fall of 1952, when I went home to pack and say farewell, everywhere I went people treated me like I was a celebrity. They were so awed with the thought that a young woman would be willing to go all the way to Alaska. It was still a very far away place, very mysterious.

I'd never flown before, so of course I was dressed in my Sunday best. I spent one night in Seattle, and while I was there I shopped for a coat. When the salesgirl learned that I was going to Alaska, she called all the other clerks over, to come and have a look at me. That really took me by surprise, that even in Seattle they obviously didn't see many women going to Alaska. Some knew of a friend or relative there, or someone married to a military man, but to want to go up there and work? They couldn't imagine that.

I took the steamship to Juneau, then flew on to Anchorage. The next day I took a small plane to Seward. It still makes me laugh, to think of myself climbing into that little plane, wearing my veiled hat and high heels.

To celebrate my arrival, all the available children and staff from the Jesse Lee Home came to the airport to greet me. It was very touching. The superintendent's wife introduced herself and told me that, with my arrival, their staff was complete for the first time. She also told me that, instead of the nursery boys I was hired to take care of, I was being assigned the school-age boys. That threw me into a panic; I felt that I was completely in over my head. But as soon as I got to know the boys, I discovered they were a delightful bunch.

By the time I got to Jesse Lee, they had stopped teaching within the home. That was a disappointment for me. The city limits had been revised, and the Jesse Lee kids were now being bussed to Bayview Elementary and Seward High, which was good for them, because they needed to mingle with the town kids. So instead of teaching, I did a lot of laundry, sewing, ironing and patching clothes.

Betty Epps in Seward, 1952

The facility consisted of three buildings. There were approximately 100 people living there, including 14 staff members. The middle building was the dining room and kitchen, with a heating plant downstairs and a big library upstairs. The girls building had three dorms, with each dorm housing 10 or 12 girls. The boys building sat at the opposite end of the compound, and had four dorms. When I say a dorm, I'm talking about a huge room with single beds lined up along the walls and chests of drawers between each one. I had my own little room, of course.

The kids were mostly Natives; we had a mixture of Athabascans and Eskimos and Aleuts, with a smattering of white kids. Very few of them were truly orphans; most had one parent somewhere, who for some reason could no longer take care of them. The parents didn't want to give them up for adoption, though. They were holding onto the hope that someday they could become a family again. Unfortunately, that rarely happened.

It was heartbreaking, how the kids used to wait for their parents to come and take them home. Most of them lived in a fantasy of the traditional family, but no matter how much we wanted that for them, it just wasn't going to happen.

I quickly settled into life at the home. The wake up bell rang at 6:15. The children would stand in line for cod liver oil, then tromp down the long corridor to the dining room. After breakfast they would scurry to get their chores done before school. The daily routine was basically the same, with specific household duties assigned to each child and rotated on a monthly basis.

My boys were all school age, so they were gone on week days. On weekends we would go to the beach or the movies. On Sundays we would all pile into the back of the old Jesse Lee truck and arrive en masse at the Methodist Church. We often had picnics on Sunday afternoons. The kids had a favorite spot where they loved to sit under the railroad bridge. There was plenty to keep the kids busy. There was a gymnasium built into the boys house. Lots of them became involved in school athletics, scout troops and 4H.

Each dorm had relief house parents, so we had a day off each week. We also got a couple nights and one Sunday off a month. Fortunately, I had my days off with Phyllis Dowling, who loved to have a good time. She was a wonderful square dancer, so I joined the square dance club. Even though I wasn't much of a dancer, I had a lot of fun.

In 1954 a young man, Russ Arnett, came to town. He had been the U.S. Commissioner in Nome, but he wanted to see what other communities in Alaska were like. He had a law degree but he decided to try something else for a while, so he got a longshoreman's job. On our first date we biked out to an old logging camp outside of town, by a little lake, and had a picnic. We dated from then on, and got married at the end of my second year at the home.

Russ decided to return to his law career, and we ended up living in Anchorage. I stayed at home to raise our three children, then taught kindergarten at various Anchorage schools for about ten years. We consider ourselves very lucky; our children and grand-children have chosen to remain in Alaska. Last June, I celebrated my 70th birthday by climbing the Chilkoot Trail with my son, Hans, and daughter-in-law, Reinet. I hike and ski with a group of girls my age, and they had done the Trail when they were younger. I took one of them aside and asked her if she thought I could do it, and she said yes, but that I'd need to train.

I got lots of help from the senior center and trained all winter. I practiced with weights on my back, climbing around on the trails around town; I was out there every day. And it's a good thing too, because I couldn't have done it if I hadn't worked out all winter.

Going over the Chilkoot Trail was one of the highlights of my life. Another highlight was working at the Jesse Lee Home. I sure hope the efforts to restore the Home's remaining building are successful. I know that would mean a lot to a whole lot of people.

Daisy Lee Bitter

Daisy Lee Andersen was born on a farm in California's San Joaquin Valley. By age six she was driving a mule team and the family tractor on a regular basis. As the oldest child, she was soon "promoted" to helping her father with the heavier chores, which included working a gold mining claim in the Sierra Nevadas.

Her Depression era childhood wasn't all hard work. An uncle with a love of botany and geology regularly included her on field trips to explore extinct volcanoes and gather fossils and plants. These experiences lead to her lifelong passion for natural science.

There was never much money in our family; we had to work hard to get by. Even so, my parents placed high emphasis on education, and with part-time jobs I graduated summa cum laude from Fresno State College. I later got my Master's Degree from Alaska Methodist University. I taught in small country schools in California and in 1945 I met my husband, Conrad (Connie) Bitter. He was an outdoorsman and, having been in Dutch Harbor during World War II, always wanted to return to Alaska.

We stayed in California for several years, but the idea of Alaska kept haunting Connie, so in 1954 we headed up the highway in a one-ton Diamond T pickup pulling a 30' house trailer. Connie got a job in the freight department at Sears, a big rambling store on G Street, and within a year he was managing the place. I started teaching at Denali Elementary School but, due to low enrollment, was soon transferred out to Woodland Park. Over a period of nine years I taught at several of the elementary schools, plus Wendler and Romig junior high. I was also principal for many years, at Fairview and Susitna elementary schools.

I loved teaching, period, but natural science was my favorite. I kept my expectations high and tried to approach learning as creatively as I could, and to use methods that were proven to work well. Instead of telling students how something works, you set up a situation where they have to figure it out for themselves. That way it's more motivating, and they're more apt to remember it.

Since few families could afford them in those days, I was prone to having lots of classroom animals: fish, hamsters, snakes, that sort of thing. When the '64 earthquake ripped open their cages, the hamsters migrated down to the garbage room, behind the kitchen, and by the time we found them they were really fat.

At Romig I had snakes. I borrowed a boa constrictor from a friend of mine, and the kids really loved that. I was the only one to handle it, of course. I told all the kids, "Raise your hands if you don't want me to come near you." I didn't want to scare any of them. I had a hunch that fear of snakes was a learned behavior. At first there were quite a few hands, and I didn't go anywhere near those students, but within a few weeks they all wanted a closer look. Then they wanted to pet it. Pretty soon they started coming to school with snakes in their pockets, little green snakes and garter snakes that they bought from the pet shop in Spenard.

We also had iguanas. The kids were free to handle them, but they also had to feed them and clean their cages. I got hold of an incubator and we hatched geese and ducks. The eggs

photo by Conrad Bitter

Daisy Lee Bitter with 55-pound king salmon

needed to be sprinkled each day, which was a problem on the weekends. I was so touched when the head custodian told me, "You do so much for these kids all the time, I'll take care of the eggs on the weekends."

I wanted my classes to be as challenging as possible. One of the students that I remember so well was Bill Granger; he loved challenging projects. He stopped by after school one day and asked me, "What are we going to do tomorrow?" I told him, "Tomorrow I want the class to learn about fluorescence. I've been trying to think of the best way to do it."

He got excited and together we set up "the great jewel theft." I got some fluorescent powder, and Bill saturated my pearl necklace with it. The next day I said, "Let's see what kind of detectives you people are. Let's send somebody out of the room." So Bill raised his hand and I sent him out into the hall. I told the other students, "Now pick somebody to steal the necklace, and let's see if Bill can figure out who did it."

Bill came back in and called the kids one by one into the little supply room. He had each student turn their palms up, and when he turned on the mineral lights, the hands of the person who had taken the pearls glowed. Of course, no one could figure out how Bill knew who the thief was, so we showed them the fluorescent powder, and then I gave my lecture on the subject. I worked hard to find motivating ways to introduce each concept.

Field trips were a big part of my teaching. I launched a program to bring kids down to Homer, to explore the marine biology of the area. The first couple years we flew down on a DC-3, just for day trips. We made other trips as well, to Mekoryuk and Wainwright, on smaller planes.

In 1964 I helped organize a statewide science curriculum workshop. We brought in two prominent national leaders in science education, George Katagiri and Frank Salamon. It was really a shot in the arm for science education in Alaska. But my most satisfying moments were in the classroom. Just after the earthquake, I helped my seventh grade students at Wendler make a seismograph from things they were easily able to collect. We recorded a couple of whopper aftershocks, the story got into the paper, and it was picked up by the Associated Press. I got letters from teachers all over the country, wanting plans for it.

I coordinated education programs for hundreds of Native boarding home students attending Anchorage secondary schools, and was the first director of the Indian

Education Program. I taught and produced two instructional TV series, one of which won an Alaska Press Club award. I was nominated for Alaska Teacher of the Year and have published countless articles, speeches and pictures.

Connie and I moved to Homer in 1983, when I retired from the Anchorage School District. I set up the first educational programs for the Center for Alaskan Coastal Studies and have been continually involved in the production of "Kachemak Currants," a natural history program for public radio, for 16 years.

There's been a lot of hullabaloo made about me over the years. But really, it's all very simple. I loved my work. I can think of no occupation more interesting, more challenging, more important, or satisfying than that of a classroom teacher.

The core of my belief about education is that it works best when the students are actively involved. I think teachers need to keep their expectations and their motivation to learn high and to always be fair. The authoritative approach in the classroom is a contradiction of our democratic ideals. As for teaching values, the best way is always by example.

I continue to reap the rewards of my long career in education, because every now and then a student (or their parents) will contact me, to tell me that I was important in their life. Boy, does that ever feel good!

photo by Conrad Bitter

Daisy Lee Bitter with a limit of ducks, 1956

Louise Kimura Wood

My father, Harry Y. Kimura, was born in Nagasaki, Japan in 1880. I don't really know much about his life, as he never spoke of it. As an older adult, I learned that when he was 14 he worked on an ocean liner as a cabin boy, and that he was in San Francisco for a while. It was there, during the great earthquake of 1906, that he lost all of his official papers. By 1910 he had drifted up to Seattle, where he attended baker's school and later opened a restaurant.

Mom was also from Nagasaki. She worked as a telegraph operator. She and Dad married, then moved to Anchorage in 1916. I am the middle of five children: Frank, George, Louise, Bill and Sam.

I was born in 1918, in a log cabin on 4th Avenue. At that time my mother had a laundry business with her sister. My parents later opened their own laundry, on 5th and C, the HNK Laundry. Next door to that, they also opened a restaurant. But times were tough, and they had to make a decision about how best to take care of their children. Reluctantly they sent us to Japan, to live with relatives until they could support us. Bill and I stayed with one uncle, and George and Frank stayed with another uncle, all in Nagasaki.

Mom came and got us in 1927, and Frank and George returned a year later. I don't recall much about Nagasaki, except that I didn't like it. We lived out in the country and had to walk from the farm to school each day. Of course, at that point I was fluent in Japanese, though I was actually bilingual.

When we returned to Anchorage, we went to school where the Performing Arts

Kimura family in the early 1930s

Center is now located. I had difficulty in school because I knew very little English and, even though I was nine years old, I had to start in first grade. Mathematics was the only thing that I knew as well as other children my age.

My mother was still running the laundry and my father had a Chinese restaurant next door, the Chop Suey House. The whole family pitched in and helped. My father was a real gourmet; he loved to cook Western style. Mom, on the other hand, loved to cook Japanese food, so I grew up eating a variety of wonderful food.

When I was ten, my brother Sam was born, and I became his full-time babysitter. He was like a live doll, and everywhere I went I'd put him in the buggy and take him with me. Anchorage then was pretty much only 4th and 5th Avenue, so all the businesses were congregated right in the downtown area. Very few people had cars. There really wasn't much need for one because everything was within walking distance.

Being unable to speak English well set me apart from other kids, plus I had to take care of Sam a lot of the time, but my childhood was as normal as any other child's. I wasn't exposed to any prejudice or cruelty because I was Japanese.

I don't remember that there was a whole lot of fun to be had in Anchorage in those days. I had one close girlfriend, Virginia Reno. She and I used to play hopscotch and jump rope all the time. The Elks used to have a picnic every summer. They'd truck us to Lake Spenard and we'd have hotdogs and all kinds of goodies. In the winter we often ice skated at Mulcahy Park.

My brother Bill was a talented artist. My parents hired a man to come to our house and give him painting lessons. The boys would also get together and play music. Frank played the clarinet, George played saxophone and Bill played the violin. An Italian family lived nearby, the Pastros, and their son Eugene played the accordion. He would come over and they'd have jam sessions. That was always a lot of fun. George was in the army at Fort Richardson when World War II broke out. Eventually he served as an interpreter in the South Pacific.

At that point, I was still single and living at home. Even after the war started and we were evacuated, we weren't treated disrespectfully. The government did send an armed soldier to our house to put us under house arrest. Since Mom and Dad had businesses, they had to arrange for people to take care of them. Everything was uncertain in those days and we just lived from one day to the next.

My father, because he was born in Japan and his papers had been lost, was taken to a prisoner of war camp in New Mexico. Our mother, because she had five American children, was sent to an internment camp in Hunt, Idaho. Those days are still painful for me to recall. We could only take 60 pounds of personal items each, so we had to leave almost everything behind.

We were first sent to a camp in Puyallup, Washington, then on to Camp Minindoka in Idaho, which is out in the desert. I had never seen sagebrush or rattlesnakes, and there was so much dust. We lived in barracks, with a community bathroom and a community kitchen and dining room, so there was no real privacy.

I was going with a young man I'd known in Anchorage, George Sawata. He was sent to the same camp and, after a few months in Idaho, he and I made our minds up to leave and get married. You were allowed to leave the camp, as long as you went east; you just couldn't go west. So George left and found a place to live in New Jersey. I joined him a little later and we were married. We both went to work in a defense plant after that.

We were still there when the war ended. When the defense plants shut down, we went to work for a yardage manufacturer. We lived in New Jersey for five years, until I got pregnant. At that point we decided to move to Chicago, where George's family lived. Our first son, Steven, was born there. We lived in a one-room apartment for five years, until finally I just had to go back home to Alaska.

We returned to Anchorage in 1951. That same year Mom and Dad went back to visit Japan, to see the devastation in Nagasaki. While they were gone, we moved into their house. When they returned, they built a big house on 13th and G, and we moved in with them; there was enough room in the new house for all of us.

After the war, my folks had opened up a restaurant, the Golden Pheasant, on D Street between 4th and 5th, where Phyllis's Restaurant is now. My brothers all helped, and eventually I did too. Then my brother George opened the Snow White Laundry on 7th and I, and my husband and I both worked there. Our second son, Mike, was born in 1958. The boys both went to Chugiak Elementary School, then later to West High.

My husband died of a heart attack in 1964. That was a very rough time for me. I was working at the laundry every day and when my brother George opened up Nikko Garden, I worked there on weekends, always trying to make a little more money to raise the two boys.

Five years later I married Ross Wood, who was then working for a local travel agency. After we married we moved to Kodiak, where he was elected borough mayor. My son Mike went to Kodiak with us for a year, but he wasn't happy there, so he and I came back, and I went to work for a travel agency here in Anchorage.

Ross was always on the go. After leaving Kodiak, he worked for the City of Whittier. I didn't have any desire to live in Whittier, however, so Ross was always in and out of Anchorage during those days. He later got a job in Barrow, for the Arctic Slope Regional Corporation. When he got settled, he called me and told me I could make more money working for the travel agency up there, so I joined him in Barrow. We were there for about five years, until Ross died in '86. But I could never stand to be away from Anchorage for long. I kept coming back whenever I could.

After I returned to Anchorage for good, I started volunteering at the Anchorage Convention and Visitor's Center once a week. I've done that for a long time now, and I enjoy it a lot.

I used to enjoy cooking, but I don't cook much any more. What I mostly do these days is quilt; I'm at it every day. I just started taking lessons one day and now I'm hooked. I've made about 25 quilts. They're nothing special, but they mean a lot to me. I enjoy giving them to my friends and family members.

My brother Sam, who died several years ago, was a well known photographer. He was especially known for his photographs of Alaska Natives. In January (2002) there's going to be an exhibit of his work here in Anchorage. As the last living member of the Kimura family, I'm really looking forward to that.

Bob Moss

I was born in 1922 in Willimantic, Connecticut. During the war I spent four years in the South Pacific, after which I went back to college. There I met my wife, Carol, who was studying education at the University of Connecticut.

My brother, Joel, had been in Alaska for several years by then, and in 1947 I decided to join him up here. The road commission was putting the road in from Kenai to Homer, and Joel was the locating engineer. There were about nine or ten of us on the crew. We started just a little south of Kenai and ended up in Ninilchik in September. That was the year of the big fire on the Kenai Peninsula. We were working around Kasilof and the smoke got so thick, our Russian cook threatened to quit if we didn't move the camp. Everyone knows a good cook is hard to come by, so we moved across the river.

Joel and I had some homestead land across from Homer in Peterson Bay. When the summer ended, we put our stuff in a dory in Deep Creek, went over to Peterson Bay, and spent the winter building a cabin. We had the whole area totally to ourselves.

The following spring Carol and I married, and she joined me and Joel in that little cabin. It's always been remarkable to me, that she made that transition so smoothly. One day she was a city girl with all the conveniences she'd always been used to, and the next day she was in a one-room, half-finished cabin, with no one else around, no radio, no nothing. But she loved it. When she went back East to visit her girlfriends, after our first son was born, she couldn't wait to get back to Alaska.

In those days we were fishing exclusively salmon and halibut. In the summer we fished and in the winter we built boats. Joel and I got a sawmill going, put a boat-house up, and over the years we built nine or ten different boats. As the fishing conditions changed, we needed different types of boats.

Our situation was completely a family set up. Carol and Joel and I all worked together, and when our sons Bob and Chris got old enough, they worked with us too. We'd leave for the summer and seine in Kodiak and Cook Inlet. It was a fun family operation.

In the early days we did all our trading in Seldovia. Those years were an interesting window in time, because we saw Seldovia go from being a real hub of activity, with its hospital and its electrical plant, and its busy harbor and canneries, to a place that changed a lot after the earthquake. When Seldovia was booming, Homer was practically nothing. Fox farming was about the only major activity, aside from fishing. King crab didn't really take off until the middle 50s.

In the winter we'd go to Seldovia once a month. We had to figure the tides just right, because if they changed before you got around the corner, we didn't have the power to buck the tide. A couple of times we miscalculated and had to turn around and go home.

To show you how times have changed: Joel and I had a rule, that we wouldn't go halibut fishing in the spring until the price got up to ten cents a pound. It usually started at eight cents, but we were stubborn and held out for more. That was our little streak of independence.

Carol and I lived in Peterson Bay for six years, until it was time for the boys to go to school. Our friends, the Lathams, had given us an acre of land for a wedding present, on East Hill Road. We built our home there and kept acquiring more land when-ever it became available.

Bob Moss near his Peterson Bay cabin

We watched Homer grow and evolve. In those early days you made your own recreation to a much greater extent than today. In the early '50s a group of people started a ski club. We had a rope tow that we moved two or three times. At first it was up near the White Alice site, on Diamond Ridge. It's been on Ohlson Mountain now for quite a long time. Downhill skiing was an important high school sport, and cross-country skiing was too. That really kept a lot of kids busy and out of trouble. You knew when they skied they'd be asleep early that night, so a lot of parents pitched in and supported it. We also often traveled way into the back country and skied there.

Some of the ways that money could be made around here, other than fishing, was working for the schools or federal employment. Quite a few people made their living that way. People also mined coal off the beach. Jake McClay and I had a tractor, a Jeep and a used trailer, and we used to mine coal off the beach. One year we got a contract for the school for 300 tons of coal. We also sold to individuals.

Joel and I got into trawling when it first started, selling shrimp to the plant at the end of the spit, which was a year round operation. In the early '70s we went Outside and bought a 47' wooden boat, the *Melody*, which we used for halibut and salmon, as well as shrimp. About that time, Carol went back to teaching school. She taught for 18 years, pretty much all the different grades.

A few years later the cannery sold us their 58' steel seiner boat, and we used that for dragging. Then it got to where dragging was more competitive, and we wanted something with more deck space and two reels, so we'd be able to put one net out while we unloaded the first. In 1980 we took the boat to Seattle and had it cut in half, to lengthen it an extra 15 feet.

When you major in fish and wildlife management, and make your living on the ocean, you pay pretty close attention to certain issues. I never felt that in those earlier days they did a good enough job keeping track of the temperature and the salinity and the kinds of things that really dictate what happens in the water.

During the '60s I was on the state board of Fish and Game and later spent a decade on the judicial council, which was quite an honor, as I was the only fisherman I know of who was ever appointed to it. I was also an advisor to an important international commission, the one that involved the U.S., Canada and Japan. This was before the Magnuson Act, when there wasn't any protection on the high seas, and we really had to actively protect our salmon. We met once a year and fought over quotas and fishing regulations. It's no longer in effect, partially because of the 200 mile limit, which we worked long and hard for.

I quit commercial fishing somewhere in the '90s, but I'll never quit fishing. In fact, Carol and I just had a boat built for sport fishing. She loves to fish as much as I do. We go out whenever we can. We troll for salmon and halibut all year long.

One of the things we really look forward to is, for the last 15 years now, we put our motor home on the ferry and go to Kodiak the last part of August. We have a little raft, and we just fish along the road system in different bays when the silvers show up. We usually stay six weeks. At night you park on a beach somewhere and, after a while, you don't really care if the fish show up or not, it's just neat to be camping.

We always have plans to take the motorhome around other parts of Alaska, and to a certain extent we have, but we get pretty busy in the spring. We put a lot of time into our greenhouse, but we still intend to see a lot more of the state, it's just a matter of finding the time. We also like to go Outside occasionally and see the spring flowers in the desert, though years will go by and we'll realize we haven't been Outside in a long time.

My philosophy is, you've gotta keep doing the things that matter to you. If you quit doing those things, then you're in trouble. Take swimming, for instance. I swim a mile a day; I've been swimming for years. I don't like it, it's really boring, but I know how good it is for me.

It has been very rewarding for me to have had a part in developing the fisheries of our state. In addition, it was a great way to raise a family and will be something to look back on in these changing times.

Mary More

My father, M.A. McCorkle, came to Alaska from Indiana in 1918. During World War I he was a radio operator in the Navy. He later enlisted in the U.S. Army Signal Corps and was assigned to a group called the WAMCATS. In those days communication was based on the telegraph system, and scattered all over Alaska were little one-man stations. For my dad's first assignment he was sent up the Yukon River to Holy Cross.

What we now know as ACS (Alaska Communications Systems) was originally part of the Army Air Corps and later came under the domain of the U.S. Army Signal Corps. So, although I was unaware as a child, I later realized that my father was one of the pioneers of communication in Alaska.

In 1919 my mother came up to Alaska to marry my dad. She took the train from Chicago to Seattle, a ship to Skagway, and the narrow-gauge railroad to Dawson. There she got the last river boat out, just before freeze up. Her journey on the Yukon took six weeks, all the way around and down the river to Holy Cross. She and my dad were married there on the 15th of September.

I was born in Holy Cross in 1921. My family left when I was nine months old and from then on we lived in various places all over Alaska and occasionally in Seattle, where the U.S. Army Signal Corps was headquartered. We lived for at least two years each in Juneau, Nome, Kodiak, Sitka, Seward and Anchorage.

We lived in Sitka for a little over three years, during the time I was in third grade. Sitka is one of my favorite towns in Alaska; I have very vivid memories of being a kid there. Every time the boat would come in, everybody would rush down to the dock to see who was coming, who was leaving and who was brand new. Among all the other things, the boat brought crates of eggs packed in sawdust and a barrel of pound-bricks of butter, packed in brine. For the longest time, whenever I tasted fresh eggs, I thought they didn't have any flavor.

We lived in an apartment right next to the Saint Michael's Church. We used to keep a close eye on the church, observing the outdoor ceremonies, which we found fascinating. For fun, we used to take a rowboat from Sitka to Japonski Island, where the naval base had been, and poke around in the old buildings.

Mary More outside of Juneau, 1942

We were living in Juneau when World War II began. After the bombing of Pearl Harbor, my mother and sister were quickly evacuated to Seattle. They later told us how scary the voyage had been, with ship blackouts on the way south. I had been Outside to business college, so I was old enough at that point to make my own decisions, and I didn't want to leave Alaska. That was due in part to the fact that in 1940 I had met my future husband, Vernon More.

Vernon had a sister who lived in Petersburg, so he would stay with her in the summers and work in the cannery. After he graduated from high school he went to Juneau, to work in the old AJ Mine. He was planning to save his money and go back to school to become a teacher and a coach. Then along came the war, and he had to put his plans on hold.

Vernon and I were married in 1942. Soon thereafter he was on his way to Nome, working on communications for the Army and ACS. I was so thrilled when I was allowed to join him there, but everybody kept asking me, "What in the world will you do in Nome?"

I hadn't given it any thought, but it turned out we were busy all the time. In fact, I don't think we ever had more fun in our lives. And while we were there we saw some of the most beautiful northern lights I've ever seen. We lived in a little one-room apartment with a tiny kitchen and plywood walls, directly above the Nevada Bar. When the wind would blow, which was most of the time, the walls would really rattle. Then the action in the bar would start up.

Everybody in Alaska in those days made their own entertainment. We played a lot of cards and went to a lot of dances. We'd go out to the movie theater on the post, which was in an old Quonset hut. I was also working as a medical secretary for Dr. Morkum at the old Maynard Columbia Hospital. Our oldest son, Michael, was born in Kodiak. Our younger son, Ken, was born here in Anchorage, in the old 505th hospital at Fort Richardson. It was a pretty rough set up; the wards were very similar to Quonset huts, except they were larger and had wooden corridors.

I've lived in Anchorage several different times. Our last move was from Seward to Anchorage in 1959. Vernon worked in the Federal Building downtown, in the accounting department of the Alaska Communications System.

When Vernon retired from the military he went back to school and got his B.A., then his Masters. He taught school for 15 years on the base, starting at Aurora and later the middle school. He was really an outstanding teacher. Not only was he beloved by his students and their parents, he was incredibly creative. One year he was runner-up for Teacher of the Year.

I've had some very interesting and challenging jobs as well. The Bureau of Indian Affairs in Juneau. Dr. Morkum's office in Nome. The Territorial Department of Health and Welfare in Juneau. The Division of Tuberculosis Control in Anchorage. Eventually I transferred to the Division of Mental Health and stayed there almost 17 years, 15 of them at Alaska Psychiatric Institute. My job at API was administrative secretary to the superintendent. I also organized the steno department and switchboard at the hospital. It was a lot of responsibility, but it was absolutely fascinating too.

Our second superintendent was Carl Bullmam, an internationally known psychiatrist. When API opened, he was Professor Emeritus at the Langley-Porter Institute in San Francisco, having tried twice to retire. We needed someone with his qualifications up here, so he was persuaded to come out of retirement. He was at API for four years. He was the most wonderful person to work for. Not only was he the superintendent of API, he was director of the Division of Mental Health for the whole state of Alaska. We had clinics in Juneau and Anchorage, and we built Harborview in Valdez. There was a lot of protest about that; no one wanted it, but it turned out to be very successful. I retired from API in 1977.

About ten years ago a friend and I retraced my parents' journey from Whitehorse to Holy Cross. We stopped in all the places on the Yukon that they had. Wherever there had been a telegraph station there would be a little building, all boarded up and falling down, but you could read ACS on it. That trip meant a lot to me.

I've been pretty much all over Alaska, except for the Pribilofs. Traveling back and forth in the old days by boat used to be such fun. I have lifelong friends to this day that we met going Outside. You knew everybody on the boat. They were small, but oh the fun we had for those four or five days. They always had an orchestra, so we'd dance at night. And the food was fantastic.

You go Outside and people say, "What is it that you like about Alaska?" and the only thing you can say is that you just have to have the experience yourself.

Chris Anderson

I was born and raised in Shell Lake, Wisconsin. Until we came to Alaska I'd never been more than 90 miles from my home. One day when I was 14, I read an article in the newspaper about how the government was sending a bunch of people to Alaska to colonize the Matanuska Valley. This was back when people knew next to nothing about Alaska. It was so far away, you didn't even think of it as being part of the country.

My dad was a blacksmith and he'd always been interested in Alaska. Our family didn't qualify to join the colonists, since we weren't on welfare and didn't work for the WPA (Works Progress Administration). Sort of at the last minute, the organizers of the project realized they needed a blacksmith, since they were bringing all these horses up to Alaska. That's the reason we were able to come along.

My mother wasn't too enthused about it. Her whole family lived in that region and it was hard for her to think of moving so far away. Going to Alaska was the best thing I could think of; I felt I was the luckiest kid in the world. My brother, Byron, and my sister, Dorothy Mae, did too. Eventually we all convinced Mom that it would be okay, and she was a good sport about it.

You talk about a life change. When that train left St. Paul/Minneapolis and headed out West, I thought I'd burst with excitement. A new world was opening for me, and I was curious about everything. There was another family from Wisconsin, the Barry family; they had some boys and a girl about my age. We all chummed around on the train and had a great time. Every day there was something new and strange. All that country, all that prairie; I'd never seen anything like it before.

It took about two and a half days and then the Rocky Mountains appeared. All those endless miles and miles across Montana and finally there were the mountains. They were was the most beautiful things I'd ever seen.

Seattle was our destination. I'd never been to a big city before, so of course it was very exciting to see street cars and all that. Seeing the ocean for the first time was a big thing for me. I just couldn't believe the immensity of it. And all the boats coming and going on the Seattle waterfront; there was just so much excitement. We were there for two and a half days, then we got on the *St. Mihiel* and headed for Seward. Boy it got rough on that water. I spent about half the time sitting on a big lounge chair upstairs with a life vest on, terribly seasick. I told myself, *if this is the only way to get to Alaska, I'll never leave.* As it turned out, it was 20 years before I went back Outside.

14-year-old Chris Anderson, far left, and his family in the Palmer tent camp, 1935

Before we got to Palmer the government had sent up a couple hundred CCCs to set up tent camps, but they weren't finished when we arrived. Most people stayed on the train for a few days, then moved into their tent. To start from scratch up there in the latter part of May and attempt to get 200 families in housing was quite a project. There were no wells, no electricity, no water, no sewer, no nothing.

We were there maybe a week, then they had a lottery to see who drew which tract of land. Then you moved to your tract and started clearing the land and getting ready to put up your house. We had to pretty much clear the land by hand, chopping and sawing. They had a bunch of old Cats to bulldoze stumps, but you had to get your trees down and cleared yourself. They set up a couple of saw mills; that's why the majority of the homes up there are sawed log houses. My dad happened to also be a carpenter, so they gave him lumber and two helpers and we had a frame house. We really lucked out there.

They gave each family a horse and a cow. With the horse we could skid in logs for firewood. My brother and I weren't city kids; we were pretty capable. During the summers we had stayed with our grandparents, and we were always out with a team of horses, cultivating corn or beans, or helping make hay. They really worked us. We didn't just sit on our duffs.

As soon as we arrived in Alaska there was a bad outbreak of measles. Eventually Dr. Earl Albrecht came up, but at first we had only Red Cross nurses and a make-shift frame building for a hospital. I was one of the first patients in the hospital. I came down with rheumatic fever and had to spend nearly the whole summer in the hospital. My joints would swell up; I was really miserable. It left me with a heart murmur and I was told that my life expectancy was about 45 years. They also advised me to choose an occupation where I wouldn't have to exert myself much. But I kept working hard, and I believe it was good for me; it built me up.

While I was in high school I worked one summer down in Kenai at Libby's Cannery. We came to Anchorage, got on an old coal barge and went to Kenai. We worked for $115 a month, and with overtime we were able to come home with almost $400. That was real big money. One year I worked in Kodiak. I went from Anchorage to Seward on the train, then by Alaska Steamship to Kodiak. Then a small cannery boat picked us up and we went to Uganak Bay. We worked there all summer and came back with quite a few bucks. I was 17 or 18 years old.

I graduated from high school in 1939 and married Dorothy Sheely in 1941. We bought a farm in Palmer, where the fairgrounds are located now, and started farming right off the bat. Since everything had to come from Seattle by boat, everyone was getting started raising spuds and other vegetables and getting some dairy farming started. We had Anderson's Farm from 1940 until 1955, and in the meantime we also had three great kids. It was a whole lot of hard work but we were young and we didn't mind. It was a good life, and a good place to raise kids. The world was a lot smaller then, and you made lifelong friends. On Saturday nights we'd either go to the Moose Lodge or the Elks Lodge. We'd have a picnic and go dancing; we always had a good time.

One year, in about 1952, we ran short of milk in the Valley; the Army needed more and the city needed more. So Virgil Ekert and I went to Seattle and Vancouver. We spent about a month Outside and ended up bringing home three DC-6 loads of milking cows. We also bought 29 head of heifers and shipped them up. I'm probably the only guy who has ever milked cows at 16,000 feet.

The farmers Outside; their cows were on pasture year-round. Up here you keep your cows in the barn about six months out of the year and hand feed them, which is expensive and an awful lot of work. About that time they were starting to fly in a little produce and various other stuff on old C-46s and DC-6s. I could see that the minute they started flying milk in, we were going to be in trouble. There was no way we could feed our cows the way we were and compete with them. When I sold out in 1955 there were 30 dairy farms in the Valley; now there are only two.

Dorothy and I divorced, sold the Anderson Dairy, and I moved to Anchorage in 1955. In 1957 I married a wonderful woman, Gertrude, and began driving truck on construction projects through the Teamsters Union. I liked working on construction because I could take time off to go hunting and fishing. Gertrude and I were always on the go.

Even though I'm 80 years old, I sometimes feel like that 14-year-old kid on the train, headed for the greatest adventure of my life. They told me I'd only live to see 45, so I guess these last 35 years are a bonus. I think that's a pretty good deal.

Capt. Jack Johnson

Captain Jack Johnson is an old salt, one of the few living mariners who can say he once sailed in a square-rigger from Australia to the U.K. by way of Cape Horn. Fitting for a good sailor, Jack has a few tattoos. The most outstanding is a "chest piece" of the Tibetan deity, Mahakala, and his consort. "Tattoos are a way of expressing oneself," Captain Johnson remarks. "I collect tattoos the way some people collect stamps or coins. But I can take mine with me."

My father was a tough Russian Finn. He and his brothers all went to sea at the age of nine on my grandfather's ships. Later my dad settled in Alaska, where he became involved in mining and fishing.

I was born in 1926, the youngest of six children. Although I was born in Seattle, I think of Alaska as my birthplace. Shortly before I was due, my mother began having difficulty, so Father sent her on a steamer from Kodiak to Seattle. We returned to Kodiak soon thereafter, where I was baptized. The priest, after a few requisite toasts, wrote on my baptismal certificate, in Russian, that I was born in Kodiak. Hence, my claim of being a lifelong Alaskan.

When I was three years old we moved to Unalaska, where Father had business at the old canneries on the other side of the island. I have very vivid memories of Unalaska, primarily that we seemed to go to church all the time. Two years later we were back in Kodiak, where I started school. When I was seven, I was stricken with what was known in those days as infantile paralysis (polio). Father quickly moved us all to Seattle, atop Queen Ann Hill, just a couple blocks from Children's Orthopedic Hospital. I spent two years in the hospital, one in an iron lung.

When I got out of the hospital in 1935, Father bought a waterfront home in the little community of Medina, a mile south of where the Evergreen Point Bridge is now located. My illness left me with no chest, just bones touching bones, so Mother got me playing a baritone horn in the school band and Father rigged a big copper tub with garden hoses, to make a whirlpool bath. A big Swedish lady would then come and toss me around in it.

Being a good sailor, Father got a dory and taught me to row it doryman style - standing - and all that helped me recuperate. Then one day an old bosun, Lars, arrived on the scene and quickly became part of the family. He taught me seamanship, how to splice wire, and to sail the dory with a little leg of mutton (triangle) sail on Lake Washington. Eventually I regained my health. When I was 13, though I was still quite thin, I was nearly

Jack Johnson crossing the equator on his 14th birthday.

6'4". Father figured that since I was strong and hardy, I'd better go to sea; it was just part of our family life. He got me a berth as deck boy on a big fishing schooner, cutting bait and pulling codfish tongues, and I loved every minute of it. Of course I was also scared, seasick and homesick. But when I got my sea legs, I was a salty young rascal.

My father died January 12, 1940. As the school year was coming to a close, my foster brother, Andy, and I wanted to go to sea again. We were too young to sail in American ships, so we shipped in the *Mirabooka*, a Swedish ship, as ordinary seamen. We crossed the Equator on my 14th birthday, heading south toward Australia.

When World War II came along, I spent almost all of it in merchant ships, sailing mostly out of New York. In the early days of the war we sailed on almost anything that would float. When I was 17, I was in the American liberty ship *Penelope Barker*, taking supplies to Murmansk in a convoy, as part of the lend-lease agreement with the Russians. Late one afternoon German bombers found our convoy. In that air raid I lost my best friend; I still have nightmares about that.

The convoy was scattered, and early the next morning we were torpedoed and sank in just a few minutes. There were five of us, wearing what we called zoot suits (survival suits much inferior to those we have today) hanging onto a life raft, when a British frigate came along and pulled us aboard. Lo and behold, that night the frigate was torpedoed. She lost about 200 men and sank. So back into the water we went, to be picked up by a salvage tug and taken to Greenock, Scotland. Eventually I made it back to New York, but I swore I'd never make the Murmansk run again.

So I went on the "romance run," down to South America in the *William Gaston*, where we loaded grain in Santos, Brazil. Coming out of Santos on the 25th of July, we took a torpedo. It took about 20 minutes for the ship to sink, but this time we were lucky and didn't lose a man. When the submarine came up, we thought we were all going to be machine-gunned, but instead they sent over a heaving line, gave us ten packets of Danish cigarettes, a first aid kit and said, "Brazil's that way!"

I ended up back in New York and shipped in another ship but had to get off in Glasgow, Scotland, as I was sick and had to go to the hospital. When I got out, the ship had sailed. So I went down to Greenock, to the sailors' home there, and sat around with all these guys who thought I was a "lucky Yank." One day they said, "Hey there's a ship for you, the *Samsuva*, it's going to New York." I went up to the lady in charge of the home there and told her I'd take the AB (able body seaman) job. "Oh that's a good Yank," she says, and she gives me all the papers and I go down into the office and sign up. Then I get down to the dock and, sure as hell, she's loaded down with tanks and airplanes and bound for Murmansk.

But those guys weren't kidding me; she was bound for New York in a roundabout way. We and other ships rendezvoused with a convoy off Iceland. We made it into Archangel in the White Sea, discharged our cargo of war material for the Russians, and back loaded some kind of ore or clay to take to New York.

Since we'd made it in okay, I was feeling optimistic, but off of Murmansk we took a torpedo and lost 17 men. Then the ship behind us went right over the top of us. What few survivors there were got picked up by British escort vessels. Eight of us were picked up by a big old Russian coal-burning ice breaker, the *Inia*. We were taken into Murmansk and, for lack of any place to stay, were put in a barracks. We weren't starving, or even close to starving, but it was a very difficult time. After a month in Murmansk, several of us volunteered and headed south, with Russian approval, and made it out through Eastern Eu-

Capt. Jack Johnson on the *North Star II* off King Island, 1954

rope. We caught up and met with American forces on the River Elbe on V-E Day.

In 1949 I was working for an outfit in Darwin, Australia, clearing the harbor of American ships that had been bombed and sunk during the war. That's when I heard about the four-masted barques *Pamir* and *Passat*, laying down in South Australia. (A barque has three or more masts, all square-rigged except for the rear one.)

Using every means possible, I drug up and headed south as fast as I could; I did everything but use roller skates to get down there. I fetched up in Port Perie and then over to Port Victoria, where I went out to the *Pamir*, only to learn that she had a full crew. Fortunately, the captain on the *Passat* was looking for some hands, so I went over there and was hired on the spot by Capt. Ivar Hagerstrand. He was one of the greatest sailors I've ever known.

We left South Australia bound for Queenstown, Ireland, for orders, by way of Cape Horn. One hundred-eleven days later we got there, a few days before the *Pamir*, so we won that race. We were all somewhat worn out, but I don't think you could have found a happier crew. Our orders at Queenstown were to proceed to Penarth, Wales to discharge our cargo. We picked up our pilot and the tugs and were alongside six days before the *Pamir*. I've always been proud that we were the last of the big square-riggers around Cape Horn.

In early 1950 I was in the Philippines, where I had my first command as master of a inter-island/feeder ship for the Pacific Far East Line. A year later I headed back for the west coast, bound and determined to get back to Alaska, but the best laid plans of mice and men ...

Instead, I fetched up in New York and shipped with the Mormac Company in the *Mormac Fir*, a World War II victory ship, then left her to join the little *Mormac Wren*, a 300' C-1 motor ship. We'd pick our pilots up at the mouth of the Amazon and go nearly 2600 miles upriver. We'd make quite a few stops, the largest being Manaus, which is quite a city. Then we'd continue upriver to Iquitos, Peru's Atlantic seaport, where we'd discharge our cargo and back-load various things. We'd have to go back down to Manaus and up the Rio Negro to a big turning basin that had been dredged out during World War I by the Germans. There they'd load us with two or three hundred tons of pure latex rubber that came right out of the jungle.

I fetched up in New York again in late 1952, where I shipped in the old *Walter A. Luckenbach*, an intercoastal ship bound for Seattle. She had eight hatches and a lot of rigging, but she was a fine old ship.

I finally returned to Kodiak one fine day in 1953 and went to work with the Navy MSTS. I sailed in a couple of their ships: the tugs *Bagaduce* (you can imagine what we called her) and the tug *Eugenie Moran*, also a small two-hatch freighter. We would sail from Kodiak out to all the Aleutians. I loved that run.

Eventually I began shipping in the *North Star*, the Alaska Native Service vessel; that's where I got to thoroughly know the coasts of Alaska. We'd go all the way from Seattle, up through Southeastern and Prince William Sound, out to part of the Aleutians and up to the Bering Sea, to Barrow. We'd stop at about 91 villages along the way, bringing them their fuel and groceries. It was a very interesting ship.

I never liked to lay around. Whenever I got off a ship I'd go to work as an iron worker or pile buck, a longshoreman or a rigger for boilermakers. I did whatever I could to make a buck, including crabbing in the early days of big crabbing in the Bering Sea, when we got eight cents a pound. In spite of the low price, we'd still have a helluva payday.

In '54 my Uncle Heinie Berger lost the Aleutian mail contract to Captain Nils P. Thompson with the *Expansion*. I was in the *Expansion* for a long time, everything from AB up to master. A lot of people think I'm nuts, but I learned to love the

Aleutians; it's such a vastly different part of the world.

The *Expansion* was a 114' wooden freight ship, Army surplus. She was purchased for service in Bristol Bay by Libby, McNeil and Libby. She had these big skegs on her bottom so she could sit on the mud. She was a very sea-worthy little vessel, according to everyone but me. I thought she was a little on the lively side.

I've seen some remarkable weather in my years at sea. One time in the *Expansion* we were running on the north side of Unalaska, headed towards Nikolski, and the fog was so deep and heavy you couldn't even see the fo'c's'le head from the bridge. Usually you can handle that kind of penetrating fog fairly well, but on that occasion the wind was blowing about 80 knots.

There were a few times I tried to work on shore. I worked as wharfinger on the Kodiak city dock for five years. I still went fishing every year and occasionally made quick trips to Seattle to get a ship. Eventually I sailed with Alaska Steam as a deck officer.

In 1960 I went into construction and, unfortunately, allowed my master's license to expire. I stayed in construction quite a while, pile bucking, iron working and so forth, but I never got very far from the waterfront. After the '64 earthquake I helped rebuild Kodiak and in '69 we were building bridges out of Cordova. When winter came on, I decided to shake out my license and go back to sea. I went to work in Cook Inlet as AB in the *Alaska Husky*, a Foss supply boat.

Soon thereafter I was given the opportunity to ship in the *Tustumena*. I moved up the ladder pretty quickly in her. I shipped as junior third mate and a week later I was chief mate. I stayed with the *Tustumena* for five years. I was just going master in her when I had the opportunity to join the Southwest pilots.

For the last 21 years I've been working as a marine pilot with the Southwest Pilots Association. It's a good job. The people I work with are the greatest. Every day is something different. For instance, two of us in the group are considered ice masters, which has allowed me to make five trips through the Northwest Passage.

In 1985 James Michener was on a trip through the Northwest Passage in the *World Discoverer*. He flew with us from Anchorage to Attu, where his wife was in the ship, which had just come from Japan. Michener and I got to be good friends. Every evening at cocktail hour he'd say, "Pass the word to the pilot that James Michener wants to see him." I'd go down - there was always a cocktail party going on - and tell him sea stories.

In 1988 the *Society Explorer* was the first passenger ship into Providenia, in the Soviet Union, though it was not on our itinerary. We were laying off Gambell and one of the lecturers aboard the ship got ahold of Providenia's mayor. He very happily welcomed us to come and visit. So the next day we arrived in Providenia, where we picked up a pilot. Then we went in and tied up at a coal dock and proceeded ashore. I did a little shopping; I could understand and speak a little Russian. Because it was an unscheduled stop and we had left U.S. waters without permission or clearance, we caused quite a stir and the ship was detained in Barrow until an established fine was paid. We completed our transit of the Northwest Passage and I returned to Anchorage, where I was met by TV cameras. I then returned to the real world of moving ships in the Southwest Alaska Pilot's region. That's what I'm still doing and it's a job I wouldn't trade for any other.

I've gotten to know so many people in the ports all up and down the coasts of Alaska. On a recent trip in a small cruise ship, we stopped in Little Diomede and Jake, the village chief, whom I seem to have known all my life, gave me such a warm welcome. (That had been happening everywhere we stopped.) The captain turned to me and said, "I swear, if we went to the moon there'd be people there who know you!"

So you might say I'm home at last. My wonderful wife of 27 years, Iris, and I have made our home in Seward these last 25 years. We love it here. Iris and I will always be travelers, but we'll always come home to Seward.

Helena Ashby

I was born and raised in Noatak, a village of about 200 people near Kotzebue. With the exception of the school teachers and a couple of others, everyone was Eskimo. My mom and dad had 13 children. We all lived in a one-room log cabin.

My father was a kind and loving man. He and my mom were both wonderful parents. I lost my mother when I was seven years old. She died of pneumonia shortly after the birth of my youngest brother. My dad was always able to provide for us. In the winters he trapped foxes, wolves, mink, wolverines, whatever he could get, to make a few dollars. Of course he also hunted caribou and fished.

All us kids went to the big schoolhouse in Noatak. There were three teachers and three rooms. The beginners were upstairs, fourth to eighth graders had another room, and the older students had the other. When I was in fourth grade the first Eskimo teachers came to our village, a man and his wife, which was really something.

One day when I was eight or nine, I was playing outside. It was quite warm, but cloudy and overcast, and I had been out most of the day. When I came inside my eyes started hurting real bad. My dad looked at me closely and said that I'd been snow blinded. He told me to stay indoors, not to go out anymore until my eyes healed. After that, little by little, my vision started to decline. I knew it was happening, but still it took me by surprise the day my sight was totally gone. I was 16 years old.

I was so depressed, I stayed in bed for three months. Then finally one day I thought,

I'm not the only one in this world who is blind, and I got out of bed. I did little things, washing dishes and sweeping the floor. It was hard at first. I got frustrated a lot. Then I started cooking and baking and pretty soon I was doing all the household chores.

My family and I moved to Kotzebue when I was 24. There I met an old white man by the name of James MacIntyre. He had lived for a while in Kivalina and gotten friendly with a man who knew my father.

Mac stayed at the motel in Kotzebue for a month one summer and he started coming to visit me, taking me for walks. He was so kind and friendly. His home town was Seattle, and when he went back there in the fall he sent me an accordion. I didn't know how to play it but I played with it, and it meant so much to me.

The next spring Mac came back to Kotzebue and lived in a tent behind our house. He used to come inside every day and help me. Sometimes he'd cook for us. He bought good things to eat; he was worried that I wasn't eating right. I had had TB off and on, and at that time I was getting real skinny. They were just about to put me in the hospital, but Mac gave me good food and stopped me from doing heavy work. I had been washing clothes for the whole family, as well as for my niece and nephews. Mac found a lady with a gas-burning washing machine, the first one in that part of the country, and he paid her to do my washing.

He was a jolly man, 70 years old, with an easy laugh, and he loved to talk. He stayed in Kotzebue until the latter part of September, then he started getting ready to go back to Seattle. I was so used to him. I trusted him, and when he said goodbye I broke down and cried.

It hurt him to see me so sad. He told me, "Helena you're 26 years old. If you want to come with me,

Helena Ashby and James "Mac" MacIntyre

it's your choice, nobody can stop you." It made me feel strong when he said that, and I told him, "I'm going with you." He was such a good-hearted man; I knew he would take good care of me.

In October of 1957 we flew to Fairbanks and then down to Seattle. Right away Mac took me to Virginia Mason Hospital to have a complete check-up. They treated me for TB and after that I was cured. Mac had four children and 15 grandchildren in Seattle and I got to meet them all.

While I was in Seattle I learned Braille. I already knew how to write and do arithmetic and all that, but I loved to read, and finally I could read again. My teacher was legally blind. She had an office in downtown Seattle, just a little place, with room for only two desks.

In the meantime Mac drove up the highway to Fairbanks and sent for me as soon as he arrived. He had a boat up there and lots of his stuff, and he wasn't sure what he wanted to do next. He thought maybe he'd like to move to Seward. He said to me, "Helena, if you want to go back to your family in Kotzebue, I won't try to stop you." But I couldn't leave him. I loved him. When I told him that he said, "Okay, then let's go to Seward."

We were only there 16 days and Mac decided he didn't like Seward. He said, "Lets give Kenai a try." We drove there, drove all around, and he said, "I don't think I want to live in Kenai either. Let's go to Homer." When we got to Homer he said, "Now this is a nice place." That was in 1958.

He bought two lots in town and built a little house. He'd worked as a carpenter all his life, mostly on big construction jobs. When he got the little house finished he decided we needed something bigger. He was 83 years old, doing all that work by himself. He'd go up the ladder with a big sheet of roofing; he was very strong well into his 80s.

When we moved into the house he decided to buy me a piano, and I started taking piano lessons with Mary Epperson. I practiced and practiced. At first it was hard work, but now I enjoy being able to play so much.

Mac and I lived together 21 years. When he was strong we used to go to do a lot of things, especially fish on the Anchor River. The first year I didn't even bother to fish, so he'd just go by himself. The next year he put together some fishing gear for me, a nice reel and pole and everything. He really wanted me to give it a try.

Mac always liked to fish away from the river, but he would always stay where he could see me. The first time I went, right away I caught a big fish. It felt like it weighed 50 pounds, and it scared me so, I started screaming. I could hardly hold onto it. He had told me to let go of some line when I got a fish but I was so scared, I forgot what I was supposed to do. He threw his fishing outfit down and ran to where I was. Just as he got there the line broke and I lost my big fish. But he fixed my gear and I started fishing again. I kept losing one fish after another, but finally I landed a 25-pounder and after that I loved fishing. One time I even caught a hundred-pound halibut.

I'm very grateful that I wasn't born blind. I have strong memories of color, of beautiful scenery, of all the seasons. I've seen lots of mountains; they're pretty to look at, especially from far away. I'm lucky, all the things I've been able to see. Mac was my first real friend, but I've got lots of good friends now. Life isn't always easy, but most of the time it's good.

David Kepler

David Kepler invites me into his home, just off the Glenn Highway. Looking younger than his 75 years, he beams as he shows me the spectacular view of the Chugach Mountains from the living room. In the foreground is the orange Aeronca Champion he has owned for 35 years. He is a gracious host, one who laughs easily and often about the old days in Alaska.

My dad homesteaded up north of Palmer in 1925, the year I was born in McCullom, Illinois. The family moved to Alaska in 1927; we arrived in Seward on Easter Sunday. Mother used to tell us she was the only woman in church that day. Her health was poor, so we never lived on the homestead. We were in Matanuska for a while, then we moved into Anchorage.

We lived on the alley between 6th and 7th on E, it was all gravel and mud. Just a little bit of 4th Avenue was paved; it was mostly boardwalks and cinder streets. The cemetery that's now downtown was about a block out of town. From A Street west there was nothing, and there was nothing south of 9th to speak of either. Fireweed Lane was just a homestead trail through the boonies. Right about where the Sullivan Arena is, there was a good coasting hill for sledding. There was a pretty decent gravel road out to Lake Spenard. People would go there to go swimming. We'd walk down to Bootlegger's Cove and go fishing in the lagoon. We used to play down in the Ship Creek area. There was a semi-abandoned homestead down there with a nice big strawberry patch.

Anchorage is where I got the flying bug. The Merrill boys were my playmates, we were all preschool age, and one day when we were outside we heard this terrible

racket. They knew what it was, so they started looking around, and suddenly this monstrosity came through the air, it was a biplane with struts and flying wires. It was flying real low. I was completely fascinated. It flew out across the Ship Creek area, then down and around Government Hill where the docks are now. From then on I knew I wanted to fly. I didn't actually do it until I was 21, but I always knew I would. Where the park strip is now, there was a golf course. It was also where airplanes landed, before they built Merrill Field. I'd hear an airplane start up and I'd run as fast as I could, trying to catch a glimpse of it. It was about two and half blocks away, so maybe I'd see a little spot off in the distance when I got down there.

We moved back to Matanuska in 1931. There were no roads, of course, just wagon trails all over the valley. Besides homes and farms, Matanuska consisted of a railroad water tower, hotel, grocery store, schoolhouse and a few other buildings. The school was fairly good sized, with the lower grades upstairs and the older kids downstairs. The teachers also lived in the building. That's where I started first grade.

Back in the 30s, everybody that could, if you didn't have a year-round job, was trapping. There were bounties on wolves and coyotes, and in the spring you could trap beaver and muskrat. When I was eight my dad grubstaked me to two dozen #1 traps and a .22 rifle, which I paid for by trapping. It would freeze, snow, thaw, freeze, snow, thaw. The traps were either buried in snow, or thawed out and hanging up too high off the ground; it was a constant battle trying to keep them working. But after two springs of trapping, I had enough money to buy a bicycle.

David Kepler working on the
Glenn Highway, 1944

The Matanuska River used to flood all the time. In 1941 it flooded on the Fourth of July. We'd been on a family picnic up at Eklutna Lake, and when we came home we couldn't get home. Dad and my brother-in-law waded in, loaded up some household goods in a little boat of Dad's, and dragged it back. After that we moved to the north part of the valley, along Fishhook Road.

When I was 16 I got a job driving gravel truck for the highway department, helping build the Glenn Highway from Sutton to the Little Nelchina River. Later I got promoted to freight truck driver. I liked construction work. We lived in tent camps, always moving around. There were five or six of us in our gravel crew, plus the shovel operator and the bulldozer operator. You'd think that a bunch of kids, driving trucks like that, would have serious accidents, but we didn't. And we weren't very careful, either; we did some pretty wild things.

In '43, one of the guys rolled a truck upside down, between Eureka and the Little Nelchina. He was sitting on the shoulder of the road, and when the boss came by, he told him, "If I just had a grease gun I could grease it; it'd be easy." He worked with them until retirement. A lot of the guys that started in those days worked clear through. We put in our time in the military, came home and spent the rest of our working life on the roads.

The best thing about the job in those days was, we did everything. Nowadays if you're a carpenter, you're a carpenter; if you're an equipment operator, you're an equipment operator. We used to build our own buildings, tear 'em down, we did all the electrical work, a little bit of everything.

I enlisted in the Navy in 1943 and spent 26 months on aircraft carriers. When I was discharged I went to school in Illinois on the GI Bill. I wanted to be an aircraft mechanic, but the course was already full, so I studied engineering. When I came back to Alaska, I did different things. I worked for the US Geological Survey as a pack mule, carrying stuff around in the mountains. I trapped on the Nushagak River in the winter of '48-'49 and worked on road maintenance in Dillingham in the summer of '49. That's when I got my airplane and learned to fly.

In summer of '50 I worked for the Survey again and that fall I got a job with the old Alaska Road Commission, building the road from Cantwell to McKinley Park, and from Cantwell over to Paxton. I did that for two or three years. I was single and earning enough money to keep my airplane going. Life was pretty good.

In 1952 I lost my arm in an airplane accident and went Outside to the Veterans Hospital in Illinois. I had met my future wife, Lois, while I was going to school there, and we reunited. We married in 1953, drove up the Alcan and got settled in. I did odd jobs for a while, then I ended back up on highway maintenance here in Palmer. I stayed with them until I retired. I ran all kinds of heavy equipment.

Everything that was used in maintenance and construction, I ran it.

Lois and I have two sons and a daughter. They're all in the area, plus seven grand-children and one great-grandson. I still fly whenever I get a chance. We're kind of a flying family. Both our sons fly, and three of the grandsons. We trained 'em right. As soon as they were ready to come home from the hospital, we took 'em for an airplane ride.

Ella Oskolkof Woodhead

Ella Oskolkof was born in Ninilchik in 1922, the second oldest of 12 children. She has resided in Anchorage since the war years, but returns to Ninilchik each spring. Over the years she has seen many changes in the small village, but still considers it picturesque and peaceful.

All 12 of us were born at home. Only one child died, at quite an early age, probably from appendicitis. In those days there was only one person in the village with a ham radio, which was how you called for help. Depending on the weather, it still might take several days before a plane could get in.

My mother was from Kenai and my dad was from Ninilchik. Mom was a little more than half Native, from the Kenaitze tribe. My dad was a mixture of Aleut, Athabascan and Russian. They both spoke Russian, so of course that's what we spoke too. When we went to school, only English was allowed. If we spoke Russian we got punished. In the winters we got our mail by dog team from Kasilof. In the summer the mail boat would anchor out and someone from the village would take a little dory back and forth. Also, there was a little landing strip, so sometimes the mail was brought in by plane.

My dad was a very enterprising person. With so many mouths to feed, he had to be. He was the postmaster for many years. He had a dance hall, where weekly dances were held, and also the village grocery store. He would order everything that was needed for the year and in the fall it would arrive on a ship. In the summertime Dad also fished.

There were four girls in our family, and Dad always had to know exactly where we were. The boys could go to the beach and wander around town but we girls, for the most part, had to stay home. Being the oldest girl, I always worked in the kitchen, where we made everything from scratch. Mother made bread at least every other day, and all the girls learned to bake at an early age. My mother made wonderful soups, and we also ate a lot of fish and moose. We had a big garden that we all helped cultivate with a shovel.

It was a happy village. Everybody knew everybody. People were always visiting one another, and any time someone stopped by you would make them not only a fresh cup of tea, but also a batch of biscuits. Our family was very church-oriented and, later in his life, my dad went to Sitka to become ordained as a Russian Orthodox priest, Father Michael Oskolkoff. He was assigned to Kenai, Ninilchik, Seldovia, English Bay, all the churches along there.

One of my first jobs was working in the Libby's cannery in Kenai with my girlfriends, although I wasn't old enough. When they found out my age, they shipped me back, but by then I knew I wasn't cut out for cannery work anyway. In those days the big towns were Kenai and Kasilof and Seldovia. The first time I went to

Ella Oskolkoff Woodhead (center) and her sister, Alice (left)
at the Libby's cannery in Kenai, mid-30s

Anchorage I was in the eighth grade. I was so seasick from riding on the tender, and so scared of getting lost; it was quite an adjustment for someone coming from the village. It still is.

Dad was insistent that we go to school, which at that time only went up to eighth grade. Kids who wanted to continue their education were sent elsewhere. I lived for a brief time in Seward, in order to go to high school. It was my first time away from home and I was miserable. I didn't stay in Seward for long, though. One of the teachers from Ninilchik had moved to Midway, between Seattle and Tacoma. She wrote and offered to let me stay with her, which is what I did. I'll never forget that trip Outside. Two of my cousins were on their way to Sitka, to attend the Sheldon Jackson School. Everything seemed so scary and exciting.

The first school I attended was Highline High, which was a huge place. Then we moved to Richland and I graduated from a much smaller school. I went to Washington State University for two years. I studied business and worked in a radio station, typing scripts. When the war broke out the campus just cleared out of boys; they all enlisted in the service. My former roommate lived nearby. She wrote and told me the shipyards were hiring and that if I wanted a job I could come and stay with her. So I moved to Vancouver and worked for Kaiser, doing office work, until I earned enough money to return home in 1944.

Alaska was considered a wartime area, so the ship had to be blacked out, which seemed spooky and dangerous. I was very relieved when we docked in Seldovia. I moved into an apartment in Anchorage and worked downtown for the CAA, which is now the FAA. Soon thereafter my folks moved to town so that my younger brothers and sisters could finish school. They bought a house on L Street, built a fourplex, and I moved in with them. The family would always go back to Ninilchik in the summers to fish and, after I was married, I went there each year too. Wayne and I built a cabin on the inlet side, it has such a beautiful view. I can hardly wait to get down there each spring.

I met my husband, Wayne Woodhead, when both of us worked for the CAA. We married in 1951, in the little Episcopal Church that used to be downtown, and moved into a place out on Garden Street. I'll always remember my mother telling me, "He's taking you out to the boonies!" That seems so funny to me now because, of course, Garden Street is right smack in the middle of town. After he left the CAA, Wayne worked for the telephone utility for 31 years. I kept busy with four children, all of whom, I am happy to say, have remained in Alaska.

Ninilchik looks completely different from how it used to be, but it's still a beautiful place. It's so peaceful. You can go to the beach and pick rocks and shells. My husband loved to garden; he'd putter around the garden all day long. One of the best things we ever did was to subdivide our property there and give each of our kids a portion. That way we got to see our grandkids all the time because they were right next door whenever we came down.

Wayne and I had 47 years together; he died in 1994. The little church we were married in used to be right where all the trees are, by the Performing Arts Center. I still go there occasionally. It's very comforting. I just sit on a bench and relax and remember how it used to be.

Jim Arness

In 1960 Kenai resident Jim Arness took a huge gamble, which paid off in spades. Fore-seeing the need for a dock in Kenai, he borrowed all the money he could, to build a dock of his own.

Privately owned docks that handle full time commercial enterprises are so rare as to practically be unheard of. But Arness, being a typical Alaskan, was a maverick. He saw an opportunity, and he went for it. Some people thought he was nuts, but he was too busy building his dock to bother with their opinions.

I was born in 1922 in West Seattle. We lived on the waterfront, right across the street from a salmon cannery, the Moen Packing Company. As a kid growing up, I spent all my time on the waterfront. Down the road just a short way was a tugboat company and three places that rented out skiffs for people to go sport fishing. A block away was where the Alaska Steamship Company parked all their ships during the winter.

The Depression hit the Northwest hard. The bottom totally fell out of the timber industry and jobs were hard to find. There were ten kids in our family, which meant ten mouths to feed. We were lucky to live on the waterfront, and we were able to pick up little jobs here and there. Starting at age 14, I worked as a deckhand on a tugboat during the summers for a dollar a day. Sometimes we'd paint the bottoms of barges for 15 cents an hour. We had our own little private swimming beach right there on the bay. We also made dugout canoes out of telephone poles, much to our parents' dismay.

In 1940 I quit high school because I got a job making 90 cents an hour, working on a dredge for a private contractor. We were working at the Bremerton Navy Yard, using a clamshell dredge to make the channel deeper.

My brother and I joined the Army in 1941 and were stationed at Fort Lewis, near Tacoma. Many of the troops around us were being sent to the Philippines. When we got orders to pack our gear, we figured we were headed there too. We got on the transport and ended up in Seward. Talk about the luck of the draw.

The Army had some kinks to work out in Alaska. There were military bases scattered all around and no way to get from one to another. So they got a bunch of boats to run from place to place, and tow barges to haul people and freight.

They went through their records and I showed up as having experience on tugs and a dredge, so I ended up in the Army boat crew. I was only 19 years old, and it wasn't long before I was a skipper. Of course, these were the days before radar, depth finders, global positioning, etc.

Jim Arness views his expanding project. Note the first Liberty ship in the background.

I started on runs to outposts on Montague Island and Outer Island, but was soon making runs to Prince William Sound, Juneau, Kodiak and Dutch Harbor. The Army started by buying a few old cannery tenders and old tugboats, and also chartering some. Then we started getting better equipment. Eventually I ended up a warrant officer on a power barge. I was on all kinds of vessels. At various times I was on an ice breaker, a big tug, and a small freighter. Before it was all over, I'd seen every island in the Aleutians and been to all ten military bases.

Our government had stored food staples at the village of Unga, in case of a Japanese attack on mainland Alaska. In September of 1943 I was sent there to pick up those supplies and take them to Cold Bay. There I met Peggy Petersen and her parents. Peggy was teaching school in Unga, and she and I began corresponding.

In late January 1945 I took a supply boat to Seattle. From there I was sent to Florida to be an instructor. When the war ended I returned to Seattle, with leave time until December 1945. Peggy and I were married on November 3, 1945 and are still happily married 56 years later.

I worked for different companies, but mostly on Cook Inlet for Heinie Berger. There were no roads on the Kenai Peninsula, except one being built between Seward and Kenai. Freight was delivered to Seldovia then we would move it to Homer, Kasilof, Kenai, Tyonek and Illiamna Bay. We also hauled war supplies from Kodiak to Anchorage. I quit running freighters in 1948 when our first son became a year old.

Squeaky Anderson had a cannery in Seldovia but was having a problem getting enough fish to operate. The major plants had fish traps which secured the main flow of salmon supplemented with setnetters. Squeaky only had seiners with a few setnetters. He started a new fishery in the inlet by convincing the seiners and newcomers to drift with the tide when the runs entered the upper inlet. I started gill netting by being one of those drifters. Seiners are not the best for drifting, but we made them work.

For the next ten years I fished for Libby, McNeil and Libby at Kenai. Kenai had become our center for work and our home. We purchased a log home with squatter's rights and in 1949 acquired title to half an acre on what became Riverside Drive.

Homesteading was the big thing at that time, and by late '52 we decided to homestead in North Kenai. I continued to fish, and in the meantime I started giving some serious thought to the fact that all the freight for the Kenai Peninsula came into Seward or Anchorage, then got trucked down.

Not able to get support from the Corps of Engineers for a facility at Kenai, I built a solid earth dock at Nikishka Bay, later supplemented with three World War II Liberty ships to expand the original facility. Docks are almost always built and owned by government entities, oil companies, fish processors, etc. When the Arness Terminal was started, there were less than ten privately owned docks in the United States.

Cash flow was a real problem for a long time, and part of our homestead had to be sold. The purpose of the dock was to handle material for the Swanson River oil field, which was in production by the time the first part of the dock was built. Drilling for oil in Cook Inlet soon started. This was a very exciting as well as historical time, and we were right in the middle of it.

We were so busy, we pretty much worked around the clock. Peggy was on the go all the time, running the office, answering the marine radios, taking care of all the details. We were so busy, we had to move off the homestead and into a little place right there on the dock.

We got to know a lot of people that we would never have met otherwise. It was their first experience dealing with tides and ice like we have here, and it was a new experience for us too. We never had time to build an office, so all the business was transacted in the middle of our kitchen, on an apple crate with nonstop cups of coffee. When oil was found, they brought it ashore and gave us the first vial.

We did that pretty close to ten years, then we sold the dock. It was a tough decision, but a good one, because I had become a real workaholic, I couldn't sit still, I was constantly on the go. We moved back out to the homestead, and that first night it was so quiet, I couldn't sleep. There were no lights blazing, no auxiliaries running, nothing going on. But we soon got used to the peace and quiet, and we finally had some time we could call our own, and it was good.

I bought an outfit that sold snowmachines and I messed with that for a couple years, but I basically went back to my first love, commercial fishing. I went gill netting, then I started fishing halibut out of Seward. I had purchased a cannery tender in Cook Inlet. It worked very well for our halibut venture too. I later bought a second vessel to replace the first, which was trying to catch up with me in years. I donated the older boat to the Vocational School in Seward. It's nice to know she lives on ...

I'm still gill netting and fish a quota of halibut with a good friend. We fish offshore or in Prince William Sound, depending on the time of year and weather. With new rules it makes sense to use fewer boats to do the same job. I setnet for salmon just north of the Kasilof River, which I work with our youngest son and his two sons.

I used to know an old guy, the last year he fished halibut he was 92. He's my benchmark; I've decided I'm going to keep up with him.

Ella Hitz Wallace

I was born in a small town in Switzerland in 1935. When I was 12 years old my girlfriend and I saw a slide show by Yule Kilcher of Homer, Alaska. We were so impressed, we made our minds up that one day we would go to Alaska.

After high school I apprenticed for three years to be a floral designer, then managed a floral shop for two and a half years. Ruth and I were still good friends. We traveled all around Switzerland, hiking and mountain climbing. After work we'd head up into the foothills and walk from one mountain range to another. We would stay overnight, sometimes in the little huts which they have for hikers. On one vacation, we went to the Alps and hiked the whole week.

Eventually we had seen pretty much all there was to see of Switzerland, so we decided to visit a different country. Ruth had another friend, Sonja, who was also apprenticing to be a sales girl. In 1957, when I was 21 years old, the three of us decided to go to Canada. We arrived in Montreal and from there we took a train to Ottawa, where Ruth had made arrangements to stay with a Swiss family. The three of us spent the winter there. I worked in a flower shop and rented an apartment. Sonja and Ruth both worked and stayed with familiies. They visited me as often as they could, and we all went to night school to study English.

In the spring Ruth went to Florida to visit her sister and Sonja and I took a bus to Niagara Falls. We'd always heard, "Go west young man!" so we got on a train and went west. We visited a friend in Port Arthur on Lake Superior and enjoyed the train ride through the Rocky Mountains.

We were running low on money, so in Calgary we went to the employment office. The lady there told us about a man who ran a bungalow camp between Banff and Lake Louise. He wanted to hire two girls to clean the cabins. We said, "Oh yes, that would be great."

It was a wonderful place, right in the woods. It was still early in the spring, so we painted the kitchen and helped with the laundry. When the tourists started arriving, we cleaned cabins. For fun, we took the owner's children hiking every night.

In the fall we took the bus to the town of Crescent and picked apples and plums. We didn't really make any money, but it was fun. After the season we took a bus to Vancouver. I went to the biggest flower shop in the city and got a job right away. Sonja found work with a family in an upper-class neighborhood. We lived very frugally and saved half of what we earned. All of us were putting money aside to buy bicycles. Ruth had rejoined us by then, and we decided we wanted to go to Alaska, to visit Mr. Kilcher in Homer.

In the spring we all bought three-speed bicycles. We didn't know if we'd really go all the way to Alaska, so when people asked us where we were going, we'd just say, "Up north."

We all had knapsacks, which we clamped on the backs of the bicycles. I'll never forget those first few miles, leaving Vancouver. We had to get used to the weight we were carrying as it jiggled back and forth. None of us said anything, but we all thought, *We're never going to make it to Alaska!*

We weren't even out of the city and Ruth had a flat tire. She was the one who knew how to fix flats, and we had a lot of them. It was quite a process. We would have to take all the baggage off the bike and turn it upside down. We'd sand the patch, glue it on, wait until it dried, put the tube back into the tire and then on the rim.

We took the Hart Highway; I think that was a new highway at that time. We usually bought food in the morning. Ruth would make sandwiches while I studied the Milepost, and Sonja was the photographer. We could make about 50 miles a day, but sometimes the headwinds were so strong, we couldn't travel that far, maybe only 35 miles. The rain didn't bother us that much. We had rubber ponchos that completely covered us.

We did without a tent until we got to Prince George. We couldn't afford a fancy tent, plus it had to be light, so we got one without a floor. The first night we had the

Ella Hitz Wallace, center, with friends Ruth and Sonja

tent, we camped on a lake. We put it up and were sitting inside and all of a sudden a thunderstorm came. It stormed and stormed, and that tent leaked like a sieve. So we walked into the lodge and treated ourselves to pie ala mode and coffee.

One night before we had the tent, there were some people at a lodge and they said, "Where were you last night? We looked all over for you." Word spread quickly along the Alcan that three Swiss girls were traveling on bicycles, and people were always very kind to us.

Someone told us there was a Swiss woman in Chetwynd and we should look her up. It turned out her husband was Austrian, and they had the post office there. We stayed two or three days with them.They were so wonderful. Ruth kept in contact with them for many years afterward. Before we left they gave us a big bag of marshmallows. We'd never had them before.

Usually when we sat around the campfire we would talk about our mothers' cooking; that was always our favorite topic. We also sang Swiss songs. At Summit Lake we made our fire and started singing, and here came a group of people from the lodge. They said, "Sing us more!" so we went through our whole repertoire again.

People were always amazed at what we were doing. They often told us, well at least you can ride downhill. But that wasn't always the case. The gravel was so loose, it took our back wheels sideways and it was very dangerous, with all the weight we were carrying. So we had to walk the bikes a lot, and going uphill we had to push the bikes, of course. We probably pushed the bikes as much as we rode them. We had a lot of trouble with dogs; they would nip at our heels. Then someone told us we should shout SHUT UP! at them, which we did, and it usually worked.

Once we got to Dawson Creek we followed the Alcan all the way up. At that time the road was all gravel, except in the towns. It was sure nice to hit a little stretch of pavement every now and then. The trip took about 13 weeks, and we didn't have a single bad experience. When we got to Alaska, we took a side trip to Valdez, where we stayed two or three days.

When we got to Eagle River, we had our customary pie and coffee. We were just getting on our bikes, and this fellow came up to us and said, "Are you foreigners?" I thought he said, "Are you farmers?" We laughed and he realized that, yes, we were foreigners. We started talking, and he turned out to be the man I've been married to for 42 years, Thill Wallace. He had come to Alaska a few years earlier from upstate New York. He was working with his brother, who made concrete blocks by hand.

When Ruth and Sonja and I headed down the Seward Highway, Thill said, "Where are you going to camp?" We said we didn't know. I had a yellow scarf, and he said, "Why don't you tie your scarf on a stick and put it by the road where you're camping?" He said that after work he was going to look for our camp site. We couldn't figure out why he would do that, so that first night we didn't put the scarf out.

We camped at McHugh Creek, and at about 2:00 in the morning we heard this roar coming up the hill. It was Thill in his old Hudson, and he was dead tired. He had been working all day, but he was so happy to see us; all he said was, "I'm sure glad I found you. I looked into every campground all the way to Seward and back." He curled up by the fire and fell asleep, and after that we always put the yellow scarf out. He'd go to work in Eagle River each day, then drive to wherever we were.

We finally made it to Homer, but Mr. Kilcher wasn't at his homestead, so we went back to Seward. It was getting to be fall and we needed to get back to Canada, to get jobs. Thill kept finding excuses to accompany us, and ended up taking a temporary job in Bellingham, because we were staying in nearby Vancouver B.C.

Thill called all the time and each time he asked, "Are you going to marry me?" I always said no. Finally one day I said yes, though I really had no idea what I was doing. At Christmastime, 1959, we drove up the Alcan and were married in a log church in Palmer in March of 1960. After that we homesteaded in Eagle River and had two children. I worked in the office of Thill's business, Wallace Construction, which later became Klondike Concrete. In the winters I worked for Bagoy's, which I loved.

On our bicycle trip to Alaska I met a nun who gave me a St. Christopher medal. I've always kept it. Maybe that's why I've had such a wonderful life.

Ebba Swanson Hamm

My father was born in Goteborg, Sweden. He was a navigator and sailor, with his own two-masted ship. My mother, Jessie Nanouk, was Eskimo, born and raised in St. Michael. In those days girls weren't allowed to marry who they wanted; the marriage always had to be okayed by the parents. But my mother was lucky; she got a good husband. They had six children, four boys and two girls. I am the oldest, born in 1911.

I was born in the town of Bonanza, which no longer exists. My dad always spoke English to me. I could understand it but I didn't speak it; it was easier for me to speak Eskimo (Inupiat) because half the time I lived with my grandparents.

When I was eight, we moved to Haycock, 150 miles from Nome, and I started school. Haycock was a good place to grow up. In those days everybody drove dog teams and the town was full of old miners: Swedes, Norwegians, Germans. They were the best people. They had no class distinction. No one in my family was ever treated with any disrespect, so I grew up feeling that all people were like that.

When I was 11, my mother died of tuberculosis. Dad hired a woman to be the housemaid and take care of the kids, and we were real close to my grandparents. They had a cabin connected to our house, and they helped out with the younger kids. Grandma liked Dad a lot. He would sometimes try to speak Inupiat, and that always made her laugh.

In the summers Dad would go out on his ship; he had the mail contract to Golovan. In the winter he ran a trading post and roadhouse. I grew up helping him, mostly

Ebba Swanson Hamm with brothers Walter, Charlie and Oscar in Haycock, 1918

doing dishes in the roadhouse. He had another little trading post at the landing on the river. In the summers we'd be out at the landing, and we'd walk seven miles into Haycock, to the (silent) movie, to see Charlie Chaplin or Tom Mix.

I went to the Haycock Territorial School and graduated from the eighth grade in a class of three students. Our teacher, Sue L. Ausley, was such a good person, she volunteered to help the three of us. She taught us two years of high school in her home at night. We studied Latin and geometry and Shakespeare, which I loved.

It seems like I was always busy. There was lots to do at the trading post and the roadhouse. It was a two-story log house, with six bunks upstairs. People often came through, like the mailman, with his dog team. I'd have to cook for them and do the cleaning. Haycock was a very sociable town. In 1920 the population was around 150, mostly whites. We had community dances on a regular basis. You'd drive your dog team to Candle, a nearby mining town, and have what they called a friendship dance. We'd stay a week and next time, maybe at Valentine's Day, they'd come over with their dog teams.

My friend Danny and I used to played our accordions at all the dances. By the time I got to be about 24, the old-timers used to tease me, that I was going to be an old maid, because most girls married much younger than that. But I didn't want to marry any of the local boys.

It's funny; I used to read a lot of western books and I always wished I could meet a cowboy, or somebody who played the guitar. Then here comes this guy from Arkansas, Nolan Hamm. He came to Alaska in 1934 to prospect for gold. He didn't have quite enough money to pay his way, but the ship's captain noticed Nolan's guitar and said, "Can you play that thing?" He said, "Yes, and I yodel too." They used to have dances on the ships in those days, so that's how he paid for his passage.

Nolan arrived in Nome and went around to the old-timers and started asking all about placer mining. They gave him advice and showed him how to do it. But they also used to laugh, to see someone just off the farm like that, thinking he could strike it rich. But Nolan didn't care; he just kept trying. He mined for five years.

We met because we were both musicians and there were always town dances. In 1935 I gave him the first dog ride he'd ever had, and pretty soon the "band" consisted of two accordions and Nolan on the guitar. We started out as friends, then I began to really like him, and we were married in '36. I'll never forget, it was 30 below, late at night, and we walked up the creek to the commissioner's house. We got him and his wife out of bed and told him, "We've come to get married." He said, "You could have come a little earlier," but he married us anyway. We stayed in Haycock a few years. Then one day Nolan said, "I heard they're going to build a big fort in Anchorage. I'm not making much money mining. I think we'd better move there." By that time we had three children.

It was strange, leaving Haycock. My sister Edna couldn't stand it, she was only 16 and she didn't want me to leave. She was a baby when our mother died, and we were very close. I asked Nolan and he said, sure, she can come with us. He had gone on ahead and found a place to live in the Matanuska Valley. He took over a place that one of the original colonists had built. While he waited for the building job to start, he worked in the Buffalo Coal Mine, next to Independence Mine.

That was pretty much the only time I'd ever been out of Haycock. A bush pilot flew Edna and me and the kids from Haycock to Manley Hot Springs, where we spent a night. From there we went on to Fairbanks, where we stayed several nights with my old school teacher. Then we caught the train to Palmer. I didn't much care for living in Palmer. It seemed like people were so far apart, and I couldn't drive a car. Having Edna there was a big comfort, and a big help too, with the kids. When we moved into the house, which was almost all the way to Wasilla, there wasn't a single piece of furniture in it. So Edna and the three kids and I went to Palmer on the bus and spent all day at Kosloski's, buying beds, chairs, a table, dishes, pots and pans, everything. Mr. Kosloski showed me his whole store. It was toward night when I finally got done. He got someone to load everything into a delivery truck, including me and Edna and the kids, and we went home. That was one very long day.

Nolan was determined that he was going to get a job at Fort Rich, the Army post at Anchorage, as a steam fitter. Most people didn't know what a steam fitter was, but when he applied, the guy said, "Oh yes, we're looking for steam fitters." So he got a job right away. He was so glad about that. He also worked as a plumber.

We were only in Palmer about two or three months, then we moved all our stuff in a big truck to the Spenard area of Anchorage. Nolan and another man, an electrician from Texas, had built a big one-room cabin for us. Then they built the other man's cabin. Settling into Anchorage was a big adjustment. Edna discovered a life of her own soon after we moved. She found a job and got a cabin with three other young women.

When the war started, the world really began twirling. We had to blackout our windows, and people had to drive home from work in the dark. That was awful. It's a wonder there weren't more wrecks. Nolan worked in the power plant at Fort Rich, and later they transfered him to Fairbanks, so we moved up there to be with him. By then we had four children, a son and three daughters. After a couple years, another power plant was built in Excursion Inlet, near Juneau. We were down there for about a year and and a half. We were back in Anchorage during the 1950s. The kids went to Denali Elementary and graduated from West High. I was still busy all the time. I joined the Homemakers Club, and that was a lot of fun.

Nolan died in '74. I lived in that old house in Spenard for 47 years, then finally I sold it. After the kids were raised, I went to work for ANS, Alaska Native Services, the first Native hospital in Anchorage, downtown on Gambell Street. I worked there for 25 years. I started in the kitchen, got promoted to housekeeping, and eventually I became the head of housekeeping.

About the only regret I have is that I never learned to drive a car. But I drove dog teams, and I married a guitar-playing man.

Stan Brown

I came to Wrangell from Arizona in 1938, right after I graduated from high school. There was supposed to be a deckhand job waiting for me, on a riverboat on the Stikeen River. I only made one trip with them, then I went to work for Union Oil Company, putting in docks. I went back to the States to go to college, but each summer I came back up, to work on cannery tenders in Southeast.

I had studied engineering in college, so when they started building the Alaska Highway in 1941, I applied for a job. That's how I came back to stay in Alaska. I surveyed along the highway for two years, which was considered essential work, so I was excused from the service for a while.

When I got through with that job I went to Oakland, California and signed up for the Navy Air Corps. I had actually applied to join before I came up to survey, and had received a letter from the Department of the Navy, telling me to report at my earliest convenience. So now, two years later, I walked in and handed them this letter. They asked me where the heck I'd been, then they gave me another physical and I joined the Navy Air Corps. While I was in training I met Wanda Ervin. We were married in 1943.

While I was in Haines working on the highway, I met a man who was in charge of the Alaska Road Commission. He told me if I ever came to Fairbanks he'd have a job for me. So we surprised him. Wanda and I showed up in Fairbanks with our first child, Jimmy. This fellow offered me a job, but he wanted to send me out of town, where I couldn't have my family. I couldn't go for that.

I used to tend bar when I was going to college, so I started looking around town to see what kind of a job I could get to support my family. I went around to the bars, and all the bartenders told me how much they made. I thought, we could live on that.

Byron Gillam had just bought the Nevada Bar and he wasn't making any money on it. I asked him one day, "Are you looking for a bartender?" and I told him what I thought it would cost to run his business. He said, "You've gotta be kidding." It was way under his current costs. He told me he wanted me to meet his wife; she was over in the hospital having a baby. I thought that was kind of odd, but later I realized it was because he wanted to get her opinion of me. We met the next day and he said, "You're hired. Can you go to work tomorrow morning?" I said, "Sure."

He made me manager right away and I tended bar for him for two years. I made him lots of money and he was happy as heck with my ability to tend bar. Later I worked in another local bar, the Past Timer. Then in 1959 Boots Newlan, who owned half of the Paxson Lodge, started looking for someone to buy half of his operation. I talked to him about it, but by then Wanda and I had six children and his offer just wasn't enough, so I turned him down. A year later to the day he walked into the Past Timer and asked if I'd reconsider at my price, not his.

The Paxson Lodge is 180 miles from Fairbanks on the Richardson Highway, almost halfway between Fairbanks and Valdez. We drove down there and I said, "With the potential for the tourist business coming in here, I could make this go." I thought it might take about four years before it became profitable, but we really liked the place. I gave him all the money I had as a down payment, bought half interest, and in 1959 I started running the lodge. Boots and his wife lived in Seattle; they were silent partners. So at first it was just me running the lodge.

When we took over the place, Jimmy was about ten and the the twins were babies, with two in between. Some of them were in school, so Wanda and the kids stayed in Fairbanks and came down to the lodge every weekend. I set up an apartment in the old building and that's where they stayed there when they first came down. Later I built a house across the street.

The old lodge was built in 1906. It was an old log place with 11 original rooms, and with the addition they put on - a frame building they moved across the street - there were 16 rooms. I used the old building as a secondary place, for the overflow. The new lodge was a frame and concrete building. It had 19 rooms, and there was a good-size dining room and cocktail lounge.

I was dreaming that I was going to fill that place up, and I did; I knew so many people in Fairbanks, tending bar all those years. On weekends we did real well. I brought my own crew in, people that I knew. I had three eight-hour shifts going. I tried to get all the truck traffic. It took me four years to pay the bank off, then I started making money. Boots was quite happy with me.

In 1963 I put a service station in. Then I wrote our local representative, asking if we could get a post office put in. He approved it and I ended up putting it in. So I became the postmaster too. We also had a little grocery store. We kept pretty busy.

We had enough kids around the area, we wanted to put a schoolhouse in too. We used the dining room of the old lodge, made it a one-room school

Stan and Wanda Brown in 1948

building for all eight grades, and Glenallen sent us a teacher. That was the first Paxson school.

During the pipeline days the old lodge burned down; something malfunctioned with the furnace. We were still using it as a classroom in those days. We'd just bought some new equipment for the school, and the trooper, Tom Clemmons, was determined to go in there and save it. I told him, "Don't you open that door, or you'll die instantly. The gas'll kill you." I had a shovel in my hand. I said, "You open that door and I'm gonna hit you in the head and drag you out of here." He said, "I think you mean that," and he backed off. That was a sad day. I remember, it was Christmas Eve. There's a little bit of the building left, it didn't all burn down.

When the family came down on weekends Wanda would help me at the front desk. Jimmy would wash dishes. There was always something for the younger kids to do. I guess Wanda and I were both about workaholics. While I was taking care of the lodge, she worked in a medical clinic in Fairbanks for 13 years, plus raising the kids. When they got older and on their own, Wanda quit her job at the clinic and became my steady desk clerk. On the maid's day off she'd do their work too.

We both enjoyed working with the public. That was the best thing about having the lodge, meeting so many people. I'd take a lot of time with them; that's how I built up my business. I had a mechanic working for me. He'd check their cars over and all that. People thought we gave special service, and that was our goal.

We ran the Paxson Lodge for 38 years. We were really proud of that place. Business kept getting better and better, but we made the decision to sell out in 1997. Boots had died, and it was time for us to make a change. It had been the source of tremendous satisfaction for both me and Wanda. Even now, people come up to me and say, "Gee, Stan, I wish you were back there."

We've only been in Anchorage less than a year. We still consider our place in Paxson our permanent home. We just returned from a trip there. The colors are so beautiful right now. The hillsides are all orange and yellow and red and green. Wanda and I really enjoy it there. Now I just plant flowers and fool around in the yard. We both take life a little more easy these days.

Gus Weber

Gus Weber, as Alaskan as any Sourdough, is also Swiss, and rooted in a culture very different from 21st century America. The house where he grew up was built in 1576, as an office building where farmers came to pay their taxes. His home town, Villnachern, was part of the von Hapsburg dynasty. Drive for any distance on the local roads and you'll see castles large and small everywhere you look.

I was born in 1921. The Swiss have long had a policy of neutrality, but they also have a highly efficient army, one of the best in the world. Every young man who passes the physical goes for 21 weeks of basic training. After that he puts in three weeks each year for additional training, until he reaches the age of 32. Then you put in less and less time until you get to be 60, at which time your military obligation is finished.

When World War II came along I helped guard the border. I talked to a lot of older Germans, veterans of World War I, who were also on the border. They weren't all Nazis. Most of them were just normal guys, and we'd pass the time by BSing. They often complained about the hatred that had been ignited by Hitler. The worst of it was the way the young people had been brain-washed. Girls and boys both were involved in the Hitler Youth program, which encouraged them to respect the party over their parents. If, for instance, a child didn't like it when his father stood up to him, or forbade him from doing some particular thing, that father might just disappear forever.

We had a million or more refugees in Switzerland; there were always people trying to escape their own country. We'd pick up bodies along the border every day. As

part of the Swiss Army, we weren't in much danger ourselves, although several times we were shot at by Nazi children. When the war ended I was hired to work as the foreman of a construction company. We did a lot of work on the autobahns, and life was good.

Weber in the Swiss Army

I married my wife, Rita, in 1953 and in 1958 we met Yule Kilcher. He and his family were in Switzerland, showing the first movie he'd made of his homestead in Homer, Alaska. Rita and I thought it looked like a real nice place and we talked about it for quite a while. Finally we decided maybe we'd better come and take a look.

It took a while before we were able to obtain all our visas, but after 11 months we were able to come. In the meantime we kept in contact with Yule. He said that once we got to Alaska we could work on his farm. He couldn't pay us, but we could build a cabin on his land and there was plenty of food.

Our daughters, Barbara and Claudia, were three and five when we left Switzerland. Each of us was limited to 70 pounds, so we took only the essentials, sleeping bags, air mattresses, tools, clothing and domestic items.

Yule picked us up at the airport in Anchorage and we stayed with the Kilcher family for 10 months. They had 160 acres, plus a fox farm. I got started building a 12' by 16' cabin for my family right away. We later moved it to town and it's still part of our home today.

I did just about every damn thing you can think of at Kilcher's. I ran trap lines around the McNeil area, all the way to the Domes. I built fences, took care of the cattle, pitched hay, stacked hay, cut wood, and overhauled the sawmill. After repairing it, I put a big log on, cut 32 feet, and I'll be darned ... that thing was only off 1/16th of an inch.

So I started milling lumber. But the safety device on the sawmill was pretty bad, just two sticks with a little screen on it. One day when I was working out there all by myself, I took a log and pushed it through and it flew back and hit me in the face. Boy, that really remodeled my good looks. The first time I looked in a mirror I didn't even recognize myself. I used to have a classic Greek nose. Now my daughters tell me that it looks more like a chicken's behind.

After the accident Rita and the kids and I moved into town. For work I did anything and everything that nobody else wanted to do. Sometimes I just had to laugh at how things had worked out, because here I was, digging holes and pounding nails, all for a dollar an hour, and back in Switzerland I had been in charge of a huge group of workers and making quite a bit of money.

Weber family moving to Alaska, 1959

One thing that was difficult for us is that we couldn't speak English. I learned some English before we left Switzerland, but I later realized that it wasn't English as people here speak it; it's what I call Limey talk.

I fished with Erling Broderson for salmon and crab in Kachemak Bay, Kamishak, Kodiak, Shelikof and Tugidak Island. We were just scraping by though, and by 1965 I was done fishing. I worked with Lee Cole, building a big log home on East Hill. I helped with most of the log work, and did all the rock and concrete work. I built a lot of the concrete buildings around town, the Acropolis building, and part of the old post office, which is Don Jose's place now. Occasionally I had as many as ten guys working for me, but usually it was more like two or three. There was quite a bit of construction going on around town; Homer was growing and Rita and I felt like we were part of the community.

Like I said, we could have done a lot better financially in Switzerland. But we loved it here. The schools were good. The kids had good friends. We hunted and fished and had a big garden. We had an abundance of nutritious food. It was a simple, satisfying life. We didn't know we were poor because everybody else was poor too.

Over the years I taught a few art classes. I never studied art, but I had always visited art exhibitions. Switzerland had three cities that were always in competition, to see which of them could bring in the best art, so we were continually exposed to the most famous artists in Europe. We had a friend who was a sculptor, he studied in Paris, and we'd often visit him there. This was in the early 50s. We'd go from gallery to gallery, walking down the Champs Elysees with a loaf of French bread under our arms. It sounds pretty romantic, doesn't it? Well let me tell you, it was.

It's been 30 years since I've been back to Switzerland. It's just too damn crowded over there. There are upwards of seven million people in Switzerland, which is about the size of the Kenai Peninsula. And you have to take into consideration that one third of the country is uninhabitable because it's entirely mountains, just straight up and down. It's too bad it's gotten so crowded, because Switzerland is one of the most beautiful places on Earth.

I was still laying concrete blocks when I got to be 70, but by then I could pick and choose which jobs I wanted to do. Now I'm retired and I just do whatever I feel like doing. Between my wife, our son, Mark, our daughters and the grandchildren, I never run out of things to do. I've always been a pretty active guy, an outdoorsman. I was a champion cross-country skier as a young man, but now I prefer snow-machining. Rita and I go snow-machining every chance we get.

Elizabeth Dennis

I was born in Pawhuska, Oklahoma in 1921, the middle child of nine. We were living in a beautiful big house in Tulsa when the stock market crashed. My parents moved us to the St. Louis area, where my mother's family lived. My father, an attorney, had managed to hold on to 6300 acres of logged-off land north of Hoquiam, Washington. So after struggling five years to make a living in Missouri, we headed west. There the family worked together, clearing land to build a stump ranch.

In 1939 I graduated from Hoquiam High and went to CPS in Tacoma (now University of Puget Sound). The following year I stayed home and worked as a cookhouse "flunky" to earn money so I could attend the University of Washington in the fall of '41. There I met my husband, Al Dennis. Al was a farm boy who came to Seattle to work in the shipyards. He'd lost his leg at the age of ten and couldn't go in the service, so he spent the war years working as a welder. After the Pearl Harbor attack, my folks were afraid for my safety in Seattle, so I moved back to Hoquiam and got a job at a service station, keeping books and pumping gas. My dad had returned to practicing law by then and had moved my mother and the younger kids to Elma, Washington, where he took over a law practice. At that point I quit my job and took over running the family ranch.

In the spring of '43 Al got a chance to come to Alaska on a cannery tender. We exchanged letters all summer and married in Elma in September, 1944. We went on our honeymoon on his motorcycle. We then moved to Everett, where we built a boat. Al worked at the shipyard and I got on at Boeing. Later we moved back to Grays Harbor, where we got into the logging business and started our family.

In spring of '57 Al went back to Alaska and located a logging camp on Tuxecan Island that was available for purchase. It looked like a good opportunity, and he wanted my opinion. So on September 1st I flew up for my first view of Alaska.

The camp was located on the west side of Tuxecan Island, at the south end of Sea Otter Sound, accessible only by private boat or float plane. There was a big shop building, six small houses where other families resided, a cookhouse and a bunk-house for six men. We decided to go for it.

When I told the kids we were moving to Alaska, they were very excited. The two older boys boasted to their classmates that they were leaving for Alaska. It turned out we didn't get on our way until December and their friends began to think they had made up the story. Al came down with a load of scrap iron on Buckshot Woolery's boat, the *Atlas*, and the boys and I, with a minimal amount of household goods, went back up on the boat, arriving in Ketchikan, then Port Protection and on down to Tuxecan.

After Christmas, we settled down to life in the rough: home schooling the two older boys. There were also the usual household chores, plus I was the company book-

Al and Elizabeth Dennis on their honeymoon, 1944

keeper and parts maintainer. Eventually I became cook for the bunkhouse crew too. Isolated as we were, you made everything from scratch, getting supplies on a long term basis, with fresh produce, etc, coming on the weekly mailboat.

Our youngest son, Jim, was 18 months old when we arrived. As he got old enough to get outside on his own, he made friends with all the people (mostly adults) in camp. He regularly visited the bunkhouse in the evening, as the guys fed him cookies and candy, unbeknownst to us.

In the long haul, after eight years on the island, with many challenges, both personal and financial, as well as many wonderful experiences, we left Tuxecan and moved to Craig. We had found out why so many 'gypo' loggers over the years had gone broke, despite the abundance of good timber.

We arrived in Craig as it was facing its annual financial crisis, the only industry being the summer fisheries and canning business. We moved into an old abandoned house where we "camped out" for the first five years. Al started getting back into the logging business while I kept house and got involved in the community. I began writing a column about Craig for the *Ketchikan Daily News*. Later I took a job clerking and managing a small dockside grocery for one of the major fishing families in town.

In the fall of '68, when our older son, Elliott, was leaving for UAF, the local school superintendent asked if I'd be interested in starting a school lunch program. I took the challenge and later expanded it, providing lunches for the Klawock School too. I turned that job over to my assistant in '71. By then we had property on Craig's south side, with a fabulous view.

In '72 Al was logging south of Waterfall Cannery when the winter watchman and his wife decided to take a break, so we stepped in. A couple of months into the job, Al got a call to go to work, welding at the new mill under construction at Klawock. That left me alone at Waterfall with just our dog, our cat and our two-way radio. It was scary, walking the boardwalks morning and night to check on the buildings and tend the light plant. I didn't see another soul for a week at a time. I kept busy reading, writing and listening to the radio.

That spring, people in Craig got an arts council started, one of its projects being a mimeographed newspaper. The 'Whale Spouts,' as it was called, had several enthusiastic reporters to begin with. As soon as I got back to town, I got involved and by '76 I took it on alone, as a personal project. I covered the city council and school board meetings, as well as the dock news, etc. Each month I mailed out 125 subscriptions. During that time I was appointed to fill in a city council term and also did freelance bookkeeping.

In the spring of '78 I got the assistant postmaster job, working alone on Saturday and during my boss's vacation, plus four hours Monday morning, distributing the mail. Earlier I had missed out twice, getting the appointment to fill the magistrate vacancy, so I was surprised one Monday morning in June when the recently-appointed magistrate and the area administrator for the Alaska Court System showed up at the post office and asked me if I was still interested in being magistrate. Yes, I was, except I couldn't quit the post office; we were heading into the summer fishing season and there was no time to train new help. They assured me that was no problem, as there was little court business and I could handle both jobs.

I got the appointment and went to Wrangell for a week of training, basically the first time I'd ever been in a courtroom. In Craig, though I was on call 24 hours a day, seven days a week, the office was open only four hours a day, and there were very few cases, mostly disorderly conduct, traffic violations and, rarely, small claims.

By 1980 the population began to pick up, with the opening of logging for the Alaska Native Land Claims. So I quit the post office and started working full-time at the court, before the job was designated full-time' in '82, allowing me to have a part-time clerk. By then I was handling more cases than the Wrangell and Petersburg courts combined. The worst part of the magistrate job was the coroner cases; the best was doing weddings.

After ten years, in which the court business escalated from 78 cases a year to 650, I felt it was time to call it quits. I had been drawing house plans for years, hoping to build my dream house on our wonderful view lot. I told Al I'd retire when the house got built, so he promptly found a good sale for our Washington property, and rounded up a crew to build the house.

When it was finished, I turned in my resignation and my office keys on New Year's Eve, 1988. Though I had dozens of projects I'd dreamed of working on at that stage in my life, we spent the next ten years traveling. Since the spring of '99 we've mostly been in Anchorage, but are hoping to be able to go back to Craig to stay.

Wherever I've been, it's been interesting to observe the goings-on in the world around me. One never ceases to learn something new. I'm still working at getting at those delayed projects and hope to have many more years to complete them.

Mahala Ashley Dickerson

Mahala Ashley Dickerson has a long list of "firsts" to her credit. First female lawyer in Alabama. First black president of the National Association of Female Lawyers. First Alaskan to win the coveted Margaret Brant Award. First black homesteader in the Matanuska Valley.

I've always loved the land. My grandfather owned an Alabama plantation, which my father eventually took over, so I grew up with lots of space all around me. I was raised in a very nurturing environment, surrounded by wonderful relatives and friends. Reading was a favorite pastime in my family. Our walls were lined with books, which my father habitually purchased.

In addition to the farm, my father also owned the general store, so we were relatively well to do. I attended Miss White's School, which was considered the best private school in the state. My first teachers were all New England old maids; in fact, I didn't have a black teacher until I went to high school.

Ashley Dickerson in 1938

125

One of my classmates from third grade through high school was a quiet and studious girl named Rosa McCauley. We became very good friends. As girls we played hopscotch and jacks, and when we got a little older we made our dresses alike and fixed our hair alike. When Rosa got married her last name became Parks, and later she made history on a huge scale by refusing to relinquish her seat on the bus to a white man.

Miss White taught us to believe that just because God had given us a different color, we should never feel that we were any less. One of her favorite examples was, she would have a big bunch of sweet peas on her desk, and she'd say, "Your mother has flowers in your garden, doesn't she?" We'd say, "'Yes ma'm," and we'd go through the colors, pink, red, white, blue, purple. Then she'd say, "Do you think your mother loves one flower more than another? Do you think God loves one more than another?"

After high school - during the heart of the Depression - I attended Fisk University, and graduated cum laude in 1935. I taught school for three years, and in 1938 I married Henry Dickerson. Although the marriage didn't last, in 1939 I was blessed with triplet sons, Alfred, John and Chris.

When the boys were six, I entered Howard Law School, which had some of the most outstanding professors in the world. I graduated in 1948 and took the Alabama bar the following year. The practice of law, I found, was quite different from law school, but I loved every minute of it. I practiced in Alabama and Indiana, then in 1958 I fulfilled another lifelong dream, by moving to Alaska.

I arrived in Anchorage on the 8th of August, a beautiful blue sky day, with the temperature a cool 58 degrees. I had tried a case that very morning in Indiana, and it was so hot; the cool of Alaska was such a relief. I'll never forget, when I checked into the Travelers Inn they gave me room #49, which I thought was a good sign, since Alaska is the 49th state. My feeling when I first got here was that Alaska was the real America, and I realized that this was where I would make my home.

Having been raised on the land, I wanted very much to homestead, so I walked down to the land office and told the woman at the desk I wanted to file on a 160 acre homestead that would be less than a hundred miles from Anchorage. She told me the nearest land available was in Homer. There was a young white fellow sitting there and he said, "Why don't you show her some of that property in Wasilla that you just showed me?"

The woman turned red, reached under the counter for the map, slammed it down, then walked out of the room. The young man came over and said, "See lady, this area just opened up, the Matanuska Valley, and these are the parcels that haven't been taken." He pointed to one with a lake, and I knew that was the one for me.

Hours later the secretary finally returned. I had my papers all ready, but she wouldn't let me file on the land because I hadn't seen it. So I took all the literature back to my hotel. I read and read and nowhere did it say that you actually had to see the land. I went back to the office the next morning ready to do battle, and a different person was there, the nicest lady. After that I had no trouble at all.

I didn't know a single person, and there were very few black people in Alaska then, but everyone welcomed me, white and black alike. The people in the valley were so nice, and all the neighbors were just terrific. In those days we got a lot of snow, and after a big snowfall I'd look out and there would be somebody, plowing me out.

I hired a man to build my place on the homestead; he did it for something like $1500. It had two bedrooms, a living room, a kitchen and a bath. I could have lived there the rest of my life, but in later years everybody started saying, "Mahala, when are you going to build your dream house?" My kids would tease me because, of course, for them there's no place that's fit to live in but New York City. I finally built a new house in '81, but it burned in '91. So I had it rebuilt, added an indoor swimming pool, and now that I'm nearly 89, I try to spend as much time there as possible.

I did have a bit of a problem finding an office when I first came to Alaska. In Anchorage they'd see my black face and suddenly the property I was inquiring about would mysteriously have just been rented. So finally I bought a little building and renovated it. In '64 I bought the property where my office is currently; it only had two little bedrooms, a combination kitchen/living room and a bath. Over the years the building has grown enormously, and I'm very proud of it. They say that blacks usually make the neighborhood deteriorate, but I don't think that's true in this case.

My son drowned in Goose Lake in 1960. He's buried on the homestead, in the Alfred J. Dickerson Memorial Cemetery. I have a Quaker meetinghouse there, as well. I was drawn to the Quakers after graduating from Fisk, primarily because of their peace testimony after World War II. I've lived through a lot, and I've seen a lot of injustices, and it's made me a diehard pacifist. That's one of the reasons I wrote my autobiography, "Delayed Justice For Sale." I didn't want to be bothered with Uncle Sam and reporting royalties, so all the profits go to charities, or are used for scholarships.

I've really had quite an interesting life. One of the highlights was when I won the Margaret Brant Award in 1995. That really surprised and thrilled me. It's the most outstanding award for American woman lawyers. Ruth Bader Ginsburg got hers before me, but I got mine before Sandra Day O'Connor.

I still work several days a week. I think the case I'm working on now will be my last civil rights case, though. Racism is a form of murder to me, and my blood pressure goes sky high whenever I deal with it. I'm just so glad that I wasn't taught to hate.

I am delighted to have lived through so much of our country's history and I'm so grateful that I came to Alaska. I never want to live down south again. Alaska isn't a utopia, especially for minorities, but it's as American as America gets. Now I understand exactly how Scarlett O'Hara felt about Tara.

Audrey Tuck

Audrey Tuck was born in 1921, in Oklahoma, to a white mother and a Cherokee father. The two families disapproved of the marriage; his family didn't like his association with a "white eyes," and her family didn't like "that Indian."

I have one vague memory of a time in Oklahoma, of being at what they called a stomp dance, which was held weekly. A huge bonfire was built, then the men, single file, joined in a circle, dancing and chanting. I remember the jingling of their conchos and the shells on their knees. Blankets were laid out around the circle's perimeter, where the women and children were observing.

Our family moved to Kansas, where my dad became a farm foreman. When I was old enough to enter school, a whole beautiful, big wide world opened up for me and for the next 12 years school was the highlight in my life. I had an insatiable appetite for learning, a curiosity that was never adequately fed, and my dad encouraged me all the way. He taught me that the quest for knowledge was paramount, that the more you learn, the more you

Audrey Tuck in 1941

Daughter Kay and her father,
collecting water, 1952

realize how little you actually know. He used to tell me over and over, "Just be who you are. Just be yourself."

In 1952 my husband Bill and I moved to Alaska and bought two lots near Eagle River. There was another couple along side us; we were all carving our homes out of the wilderness and we all worked together. It was hard work, but there were also many good times. For our building site preparation, Bill had a little garden tractor. He did a terrific job of pulling huge stumps and grading, and that fall we moved into the house. It was quite primitive, but we winterized it and everything was enclosed and very comfortable. Our water supply came from a beautiful mountain spring a couple miles away, on the bank of Eagle River, where we would fill up our barrels and water containers.

We had a real neat one-holer on the back of the lot, and when the cold weather came, we only made the trips that were absolutely necessary. It was quite an experience to be sitting out there and listening to the grunt grunt of a black bear munching on berries and rooting around.

Eventually Bill and I divorced. I was really in limbo then. I had to look around and figure out what I was I going to do. I was hopeful of getting into the Peace Corps. Then I went to Alaska Legal Services and ran into a fellow who mentioned the Bureau of Indian Affairs, which was in line with my desire to get into land law. I remembered from days gone by, it was almost like a chant, my dad had said, "Stay away from the BIA." But I shunted that aside, walked into the BIA and told them I was looking for a job. The superintendent was impressed and wanted me on staff. I said, "Okay, just pull me from the civil service register." He said, "No. I want you to come in BIA service under Indian preference."

It was the most ironic thing that could have happened. After a lifetime of being "that Indian's daughter," and witnessing all the hurtful nuances and innuendoes, here I was, about to be an appointee under Indian preference. So began my 13 years in the service of the BIA. It didn't take long for me to realize that, even though it was an agency set up to champion the Native Americans' cause, it didn't. So I made a firm decision, that I was there for the Native American, and if necessary I was willing to fight the establishment.

I married my old friend Ed Tuck and continued working for the BIA. I was privileged to work with young, brilliant graduate attorneys who came north to work for Alaska Legal Services. I thoroughly enjoyed working with them and we fought to bring to the Alaska Natives the realization of their land entitlements and their rights to be recognized. Many of those young attorneys left legal services and went into some of the foremost positions in service for the state of Alaska with the judicial system and in private practice.

One incident stands out from that era. Prudhoe Bay on the Beaufort Sea is the site of the oil industry's giant onshore facility, with a causeway leading to a dock on deep water. Construction on the land was done under the auspices of a state oil lease of unpatented, tentatively approved land, all notwithstanding evidence of longtime use and occupancy of the land (old structures) by an old Barrow Eskimo.

My co-worker took the lead on research, field investigation and coordination with private Indian law specialists. She developed the fact-finding report. Ultimately, through a long drawn out administrative and legal process, a just and substantial settlement was negotiated. Surface title to the land was confirmed in the old Eskimo gentleman. Monetary damages were awarded for appropriation of his lifetime summer seasonal home, and a lucrative surface lease was granted to the oil company, with annual rental payments to the rightful owner and his heirs. That was my friend's shining hour and, of course, I stood close by so some of her light shone on me. That was one of our many victories and it brought great satisfaction. But we didn't win 'em all.

131

Al Clayton

86-year-old Al Clayton welcomes me into his home, which is something of an Alaskan museum. Hanging by the door is a 1945 Navy overboard suit, made of light rubber and looking very cumbersome. Alongside it hangs a streamline neoprene survival suit.

The walls of Al's home are lined with dozens of pictures, mostly of family and hunts in remote Alaskan regions. A huge pair of Dall sheep horns is mounted on the wall, along with fox and lynx pelts. A buffalo skull unearthed from the Fairbanks region is prominently displayed in the living room.

I first came to Alaska in 1935, on a brief trip with my mother, to have a look at the place. We traveled on the *SS Alaska*, which left from Pier Two in Seattle. Father Hubbard, the "glacier priest," was also on board. We toured through Southeast, Seward, Anchorage, Palmer and Fairbanks. I loved it. I'd always been an outdoorsman and I knew that I was meant for Alaska.

We returned to Montana, where I studied diesel engineering, then I came back to Alaska in January, 1940. I knew there was a diesel plant in Seward, but they didn't need anybody, so I went to Anchorage and rented a cabin for $10 a month. Pretty soon I heard there was some property for sale in Spenard, so I bought ten acres. I took an ax and cut the timber, right down the middle of the property, which became 25th Avenue, off of Fireweed. I sold half and built a house on the other half.

In the spring I got a job as a rough carpenter, building barracks at Elmendorf. I also worked for the Alaska Road Commission as a mechanic, and the CAA. Then I found out they needed a power plant operator in Seward. I started that job in

1942 and stayed there all through the war years.The power plant was supplying power for gun positions at Caines Head, right out of town; it was an important defense position.

I bought a 1935 Ford; it was in pretty bad shape. It used a quart of oil every 18 miles. I only made one trip before I tore it down and rebuilt the engine. They were saving aluminum at the garage; there was a big box full of pistons, connecting rods, bearings, just about everything. I went there and picked out eight pistons, better than the ones I had, and put my old ones back in the box. When I got that Ford going I'd take my friends out. We'd drive to Moose Pass and sometimes to Hope and Cooper Landing.

One day I decided to build a snowplane, which is something I used to see back when I was in Montana. I modeled the fuselage after the Super Cub and covered it with light fabric. It had a front ski and two skis behind, plus a Continental aircraft engine with a pusher prop. I'd ride that thing a hundred miles in a day sometimes, it was just like an airplane without wings. I'd go out into a big open field and take people for rides. Kids loved it. It was a real safe rig.

In 1952 I was working in Anchorage for Chugach Electric when on a trip to Seward, I met Martine Burdick. She worked for Dr. Phillips at the sanitarium. One day a

Al Clayton with his home-made snowplane, 1957

friend told me the tides were good for clamming, so I brought Martine down to Clam Gulch. We missed the good tides, but on the way back I asked her to marry me. From then on we saw a lot of each other and were married in New York on October 30, 1954. While we were Outside I went to another engineering school, and the following January we bought a Ford station wagon and drove it back to Alaska. We had that Ford so loaded down with wedding presents, we even had a rocking chair tied to the top carrier.

We lived in Anchorage for a few more years and I worked as an operator in the Knik Arm Power Plant, down by Ship Creek. In 1962 Seward was about to get power from the Cooper Lake hydroplant out at Kenai Lake, and they were building a high line to Seward. They asked me if I'd come back and run the diesel plant. I helped install a boiler and stack, and got the plant ready to be kept on standby.

It was the funniest thing, I'd been away from Anchorage for almost a year, and when I drove into my place, right behind me there was another car. It was somebody that wanted me for a month's worth of jury duty. All along I'd been getting deferments because of my job, so I thought I'd better just do it and get it over with.

That was the most unusual month I've ever put in. We reported in at the old federal building, and everything was so mixed up, it was incredibly inefficient. Day after day, nothing was accomplished. We'd just get settled in one room, and pretty soon a guy would come and tell us that this was his room that day. So we would move out into the hall, and the men would sit on the floor. They didn't even have chairs for the women. Finally it was getting to be hunting season, so I talked to the people in charge and told them, "I have to go moose hunting to get my winter meat." And they let me off.

I always hunted moose in the Glennallen area, and while I was up there one year I applied for a diesel job. I became mechanic and chief operator and we stayed there 25 years. In seven years we had four kids: Maraley, Jeanette, Shirley and Alfred Jr. We had just gotten settled in Glennallen, then the big earthquake of '64 hit. It shook our house right off its foundation. There was an eight-inch crack all the way under the house.

Martine was home with the kids, but luckily nobody was hurt. That afternoon I had taken my snowplane and gone 17 miles to Crosswind Lake for a weekend of fishing for lake trout. I was cutting a hole in the ice, just punching through, when the earthquake hit. The first sensation I had was of being lifted up and set down again. Then the ice started cracking everywhere. It would open up, then come together, squirting water into the air, which came down as spray. That was a pretty big shaker. I hung onto that snowplane for all I was worth.

Every year I got 30 days paid leave at the power plant and, with other holidays, I'd get about a month and a half off at a time. I had gotten my registered guide's license back in 1953 and had been making a lot of hunting trips with Lee Hancock and various other outfitter master guides. We hunted in the Mentasta Mountains and the Talkeetna Mountains. Sometimes we'd go all the way to Unimak Island, or to the Nutzotin Mountains in the Snag River country, near the US-Canadian border.

As we sit in the warm coziness of Al Clayton's home, one particular picture catches my eye. I jump up to investigate and, sure enough, the subject is who I thought it was.

I've always had an interest in aviation. I just so happened to be at the Seattle airport in 1935 and I saw this beautiful airplane. I had to take a picture of it. Later I found out it was Amelia Earhart's Lockheed Electra, the one she was lost in. That's her right there.

Rica Swanson

I was born in Finland in 1905. In 1906 my father came to Alaska to work for the Treadwell Mining Company in Douglas. At that time Douglas was quite a boomtown, a hurley-burley place with all kinds of excitement. In 1908 my father sent money for me, my younger brother John, and our mother to join him. John was still a baby at the time.

We traveled from Helsinki to Liverpool, where we boarded a steamship for New York. We had very little money, so we had to travel steerage. We were all herded together in the bottom of the ship, and it was a very rough crossing. As I recall, it took about a week. We landed in New York and were met by a Finnish interpreter who corralled us all around the city. Of course, none of us spoke a word of English. From New York we took a train to Seattle and then the boat to Douglas.

I'll never forget our arrival in Douglas, which was early one spring morning. My aunt ran a laundry, and apparently it was quite a successful one because she had a lot of people working for her. One of her most trusted employees was a black man who happened to speak Finnish, so she sent him down to the dock to pick us up. When he told my mother that he was there to take us to our aunt's home, I was so afraid. I'd never seen a black man before.

He proved to be a very fine fellow. He took us to my aunt's and then on to another place where my dad had already purchased a place for us to stay. So we huddled down and got acquainted with a few of the people around us. There were Slavonians, Greeks, all kinds of people. I never understood why, but there was a feeling of racism against the Finns. Later, when I had children of my own, I didn't teach them the Finnish language because of that early experience.

The school in Douglas was fairly big, a three-story building with several teachers. The high school was on the top floor and we had recess in the basement. I'll always remember how astonished I was, to see water coming out of an odd contraption, which I learned was called a water fountain. It took a while, but I finally learned English. Additionally, all during my school years my parents paid for me to take violin lessons. I was forever being called upon to play solos at PTA meetings and so forth. At first I was so nervous, playing in public, but gradually I got used to it and I came to enjoy it very much.

I graduated from high school in 1924 and decided I was going to be a teacher, so I left Alaska for three years and attended a teacher's college in Bellingham. My brother Johnny paid my way through college. He was a musician too. He played the accordion beautifully and was in constant demand.

In the summers I lived with my parents and worked, playing violin at the Palace Theater in Juneau. This was back in the days of silent movies, and they needed musical accompaniment. There were only four instruments in the orchestra: drums, bass fiddle, violin and piano. Over time the four of us became good friends.

Every time a new movie arrived, we were given a script, which contained the music and notes about the story. We had to follow the action as it progressed on the screen, which meant we were constantly changing the music to match the mood of the picture. We never had an opportunity to watch it ahead of time, in order

Frank and Rica Swanson with their sons Dick and Doug, in Anchorage, 1938

137

to rehearse. We just played along and did the best we could.

There was no bridge across the inlet then; I had to take a ferry back and forth to Juneau. It was always after midnight when I came home, but I was never afraid. I had my fiddle case with me and I figured that, if I had to, I'd use it to whack anybody that bothered me.

I left Southeast and worked as a teacher for seven years. My first job was in Wasilla. From there I went to Fort Gibbon for two years, then to Haines for another two years. Eventually I went to Anchorage. I had met several people who lived there and I was old enough then to be a little more adventurous.

While I was in Anchorage, I was called back to work in Wasilla, which was fine with me. I had developed an affection for the town. And lo and behold, almost as soon as I moved back, I met an extremely charming man, Frank Swanson. Anyone will tell you, he was really a fine man. He was square; he wouldn't cheat anyone out of a nickel. I usually took my meals at the roadhouse, which is where I met Frank. There were dances at the roadhouse every weekend and Frank played saxophone in the band. Before long I was playing my fiddle along with them.

In December of 1933 the school sent me to buy Christmas presents for the children. Frank drove me to Anchorage and, after we had done the shopping, he dropped me off at the hairdresser's while he did some errands. What a surprise it was, when he came back to the hairdresser's, where I was sitting under the dryer. He came in, kneeled down in front of me and said, "Will you marry me?" I said, "You're kidding." He told me no, that he wasn't kidding, that he was serious. I was so dumbfounded, I didn't say anything for a while. Then we went to the justice of the peace. It was a few minutes before six o'clock, so we were barely in time. The justice got his wife to be the the witness, and that was that.

In those days teachers were not allowed to be married, so I didn't tell anybody until school was over. Frank's uncle knew, because Frank lived with him, and eventually word got around. Our friends gave us a shivaree. They stuffed the chimney and smoked us out of the house. That was the tradition in those days.

So my teaching career came to an end, and I was lucky I didn't get punished because I had broken the law. But we were free to live as a married couple, so we bought a little cabin, where Teeland's is located now. We had to get our water from a well half a block down the street, but that was no problem.

Later we moved to Anchorage and Frank got on with the railroad as a clerk, overseeing all the materials that were coming in. I clerked for Northern Commercial Company at their store on 4th and H. This was the middle '30s, early '40s. I worked for NCC for 10 years. After that I was a homemaker, busy raising four kids. Frank continued to play the saxophone. He and his brother-in-law and another fellow put together a group called the Swanson Swingers. They played at every kind of dance, high school dances, square dances, it didn't make any difference.

During the war, Anchorage was a whirlwind of activity. The town changed so much during those years, it was hard to believe. We lived in a little house on 2nd Street, right downtown. Frank was kept busier than usual with his job and time went so fast, our children were grownup before we knew it. When Frank retired from the railroad we bought a motor home and went on a long trip, all around the country. Motorhomes were new in those days; we were only about the second people we knew who owned one.

I think I'm very lucky, to have come from so far away and to have landed in this little corner of the world. My parents were hard working foreigners with four children who did the best they could with what they had. In my opinion they did an excellent job. I had work that I loved, and music wherever I went. I had a good husband, a wonderful man. I have good friends, some of whom I have known for many decades. All four of my children have remained in Alaska, as well as my 15 grandchildren. Yes, I've been very lucky.

Mabel Ivanoff Spencer

I was born in 1911 in Hope. My mother was of Russian Aleut descent, from Ninilchik. My father, Mikar Ivanoff, was also Russian. I'm the third in a family of many children. I never knew either of my folks. When I was three years old it was discovered that I couldn't walk properly, so a nurse took me to Seattle on the Alaska steamship *Alameda*, where I was admitted to the Children's Orthopedic Hospital. There it was discovered that I had TB in my right knee.

I lived in the hospital for several years. The doctors tried different things, including having me lay in bed with weights hanging from my knee. I wore a cast for a while. Finally they decided my leg would never be any good, that I would just have to live with a stiff knee.

When I got out of the hospital I moved into the Washington Children's Home and began the fourth grade in public school. There was another girl in the children's home who had a bad leg. One of the matrons always called us the "two lame ducks." We had a lot of chores, and they were very strict in the home. Whenever we did anything wrong, they'd march us into the building, sit us down on a bench, make us fold our hands and be silent for an hour. Breakfast was always cornmeal mush, which I hated, but you had to eat every speck.

There were 12 girls at one end of the hall and 12 at the other end, with the matron's room and a locked door in between. One night another girl and I climbed out the window and walked in the gutter, hanging onto the roof, then climbed into the other girls' room. The matron heard us talking and telling ghost stories, so she came rushing in. She couldn't imagine how we'd gotten there. She made us get dressed, right then and there, and go downstairs and mop the hall. There was a separate wing of the home for the boys, and we girls were never allowed to speak to them. We weren't even allowed on the playground at the same time.

One day I made my mind up to run away. That night I snuck down the stairs and out the back door. I didn't have any money and there was no place to go, so I went to a nearby park. It was summertime, so I lay down on a bench and went to sleep. In the morning, since I couldn't think of what else to do, I went back to the home. Of course I got quite a lecture, and they made me sleep in the infirmary for a week.

When I finished 8th grade, I was invited to live with Miss Larabie, a teacher and the principal of Wallingford School. While I lived with her I attended Roosevelt High School. Later I lived in Edgewood with a lady named Mrs. Lowry. She had three other girls from Alaska staying with her, all part Native. We had a house tent where we slept, and Mrs. Lowry taught us all to cook.

One of the girls, Nellie, and I attended Fife High School. Nellie drove a Model T, the kind you had to crank. We'd go to Tacoma to shop, then call Mrs. Lowry on the phone and beg her to let us go to a movie. She'd always say, "No, you girls have to come home right now." But we'd plead with her and she always gave in. She was real good to us. When it came time for graduation, we sewed our own dresses on a treadle machine that you pumped with your feet. I made mine with a plunging neckline, but Nellie altered it, to make it less revealing.

Rosie Ganungnun and Mabel Ivanoff Spencer
in Unalakleet, late 1930s

I also lived for a while in Richmond Heights with a retired army officer and his family. They lived close to Echo Lake, where I used to swim. I was always embarrassed because I had the worst old-fashioned swim suit, not at all modern like the other girls had.

I came back to Alaska when I was 18. The first place I went was Buckland, about 70 miles from Kotzebue. Tony Jewel was the principal and head teacher of the little school there. I helped with the younger kids. They always called me "teacher," but I wasn't accredited. I stayed there one year, then went to Bethel. Miss Martin was the principal in Bethel, and there were several teachers at the school. I was paid a small stipend and my housing was furnished. I got such pleasure from teaching kids to read; some of them learned so fast!

Altogether I spent 10 years teaching in various villages: Buckland, Bethel, Akiak, Eek, Kwethluk. I spent a year in some places and longer in others. The last school I was at was Unalakleet, way up north. They had a schoolhouse with quarters for the teachers. The village men used to bring wood for the 50-gallon tank stoves, for heating the school. There was no water, so they'd saw big blocks of ice from the river and we'd melt it.

I taught the girls to swim in the Bering Sea. On warm days we'd swim in the slough, in the shallow spots, but we never stayed in for very long. I sewed two-piece bathing suits for all the girls and myself. At that time there were a half dozen stores in Bethel and a long wooden sidewalk stretching all the way through the village, back to the tundra. One time Mr. Muncher got a whole box of red silk stockings in at his store, and I couldn't resist buying a pair. Then someone ruined it by telling me, "Only hurrah girls wear red silk stockings." I had a good friend in Unalakleet, Rosie Ganungnun. Her father was well known for helping with the serum run to Nome. She and I would order patterns, then get together and sew dresses.

I left Unalakleet in 1940 and married shortly after arriving in Anchorage. My son, Peter, was born in 1942. My husband was a bartender, and during World War Two I went to work in the Sourdough Saloon. I was in charge of the shooting gallery, where the target was Hitler's face. You got three .22 shots for a quarter. I learned to be a pretty good shot from working there.

I later remarried, and my new husband decided he and Peter and I should drive down the Alcan Highway to Wallace, Idaho, where his sister lived. We were Outside for several years, but I always wanted to come back to Alaska, so we did. When we got back to Anchorage he and I went our separate ways. I lived with my sister, Doris, for a while then went to work for a family for many years as a live-in housekeeper.

When Peter grew up and left home, I got involved with the foster grandparents organization. They have many different programs, all for people with low incomes. Some of the volunteers worked in API, some worked in the library, some went into homes. They sent us anywhere we were needed. I spent a lot of time in Nunaka School and Fairview School. We wore red jackets with FGP stitched on them, and all the students called us Grandma. I was with the foster grandparents long enough to earn a 19-year pin.

I always had problems with my right leg. When I started getting older it began to bother me more and more. I started using a cane, then I had to go to crutches. Then I began having problems with my left leg, and a year and a half ago they both had to be amputated.

I really enjoy living at the Heritage Place Nursing Facility here in Soldotna. We have a good activity program and craft sessions here. I keep busy. I'm nearly blind, but I can still read a little. Mostly I listen to books on tape. I like word games. I like to listen to stories and poetry on cassette. I recite poetry sometimes, and I write poems. My favorite ones to recite are "The Schooner Hesperus" and "The Childrens' Hour."

How do I keep from not getting depressed? Well you can't go around moaning and crying; it doesn't do any good. When I see someone who can't think or speak, or someone who can't get out of bed, I'm thankful to be able to do the things I can do. And I still have family members nearby. They come and visit me. I've lost a lot in this life, but I'm still happy.

Dr. Joshua J. Wright

Dr. Joshua J. Wright is an easy-going man with a fine sense of humor. When we met for breakfast recently, it was at an hour I usually sleep through. It was his only free time, he explained, and all too soon he was on his way to work. A longtime Anchorage resident, Dr. Wright has provided the city with not only his dental skills but also a love of community service and philanthropy that have benefited many over the years. His diversity and hard work have enabled him to become one of Anchorage's most prominent citizens.

I was born in Georgetown, South Carolina. After finishing high school I spent 22 months in the Navy. I then went to college at Howard University, where I also attended dental school. I worked at the post office for five years, putting myself through school.

There were three of us who were buddies in dental school and we toyed with the idea of practicing together. One day one of them told me they were hiring dentists in Alaska. I inquired and was told that all I needed was any state license. I took the South Carolina State Board, passed it, wired the Director of Public Health in Juneau and he wired me back, asking, "When can you leave?" I said, "In 24 hours." That was the summer of 1956. I was a bachelor, so about a week later I came to Alaska. I must say, I was stunned by the beauty of the region. It was totally different from anything I'd ever experienced before.

I had orientation in Juneau, then I went to Mt. Edgecumbe Native Services Hospital in Sitka. I was in charge of all children in the hospital under the age of 12, plus all the students at Mt. Edgecumbe School. I worked extremely long days, frequently through lunch or dinner. I averaged about ten or 12 emergencies every morning, before I got started on my regular schedule. I believe there were two reasons I was kept so busy: the absence of regular dental care in the villages and the introduction of a new diet that was high in sugar and carbohydrates.

My wife, Lillie, and I met in Sitka, where she was working as a registered nurse at the hospital. Shortly after we married I resigned and we moved to Anchorage. All three of our children were born at the old Providence Hospital on L Street. In those days almost everyone lived downtown. If you lived out farther than where Sears is now, you were in the country. When we came here most blacks lived in Fairview and the flats, where the Sullivan Arena is now.

Dr. Joshua Wright and his family in Anchorage, early 1960s

When we first arrived we spent about 10 days with our good friend, Blanche McSmith. Blanche was the first black to serve in the Alaska Legislature. She lived on Cordova between 3rd and 4th. With her assistance we were able to find an apartment near where the Holiday Inn is now, about six blocks from my first office on 3rd and E Street.

My practice was busy from day one, and 40 years later I'm still busy. I had a difficult experience at a local bank in our first years here, but later they ended up being a big supporter of mine. Their support became invaluable when I started dabbling in real estate.

Eventually I got involved in dental politics. In 1962 I was appointed to the Dental Examiner's Board. In 1967-68 I was not only the president of the Alaska Dental Society, but also the chairman of the Dental Board of Examiners, which to the best of my knowledge has never happened in this country before.

In 1969 I was elected to the Anchorage School Board. The number one priority of the school board at that time was to increase the education budget. Anchorage school teachers got a 25% raise right off the bat and for a long time, until maybe 10 or 15 years ago, that's how we were able to attract teachers: we had the best pay and benefits.

Of course, having come from a family with four teachers, I'm biased, but I have no doubt that teachers and nurses are among the poorest paid workers. It is unfortunate that they have to go on strike periodically to get decent wages. Most of them are extremely dedicated, and if we didn't have these dedicated professionals our system would not be a success. These days, the field can't attract committed young people the way it used to. Even if the pay were better, the working conditions would dissuade many of them. They have virtually no control over the students and, in my opinion, many of the administrators are out of tune with today's educational issues.

In 1970 I was elected to serve in the legislature. I was chairman of the sub-committee on education, which at that time controlled 46% of the state budget. Fortunately, because of my school board activity, even the chairman of the senate would defer to my experience and budgeting knowledge.

Due to my commitment in Juneau, I only practiced about five to seven months out of the years during 1970-1980. It was just enough to take care of the staff and pay the rent while my reliable associate helped me with my patients' needs. I also became very involved with real estate.

In 1974 I ran for the senate and lost by 80 votes, so I decided I would pack up and go home. Lillie was delighted that I lost that election. It enabled us to do quite a bit of traveling abroad, once our children were off to college. When the children went Outside they swore they were never coming back, they were tired of so much ice and snow. But, as all parents know, they always come back. Lillie and I are now raising three grandchildren, a commitment which has energized both of us.

I've been a dentist a long time. One of my proudest moments was in 1971, when I was appointed the most outstanding alumni of Howard University Dental School after 15 years. I acquired that status before many of my professors.

I always laugh when I recall one particular incident from the early days. A lady made an appointment with me and when she came in she said, "Is Dr. Wright black?" Lillie was working at the desk and she said, "The last time I saw him he was black." The woman explained that the reason she asked was that she was familiar with my reputation and she wanted to make sure it was me. She went on to say that her children had had such a good experience with a black pediatrician in Iowa, prior to being in Alaska, that she wanted to take them to a black dentist. In fact, one lady in the early days said the reason she came to me was that, since there was so much prejudice, she figured that if they'd given me a license I was probably a pretty darn good dentist.

I have always loved the practice of dentistry. I believe my reduced schedule between 1970 and 1980 allowed me to escape burnout symptoms. My long-term goal is to continue to provide our patients with quality care. I am blessed with great patients and a truly dedicated staff. Retirement is not part of my vocabulary.

Charlotte Allen Rogers

Charlotte Allen Rogers was born and raised in West Virginia. Her beloved Uncle Jess, who had come over the Chilkoot Trail in 1898 at the age of 18, wrote many letters home, tantalizing his young niece to dream of someday making her own journey north.

Charlotte was a senior in high school when World War II began and a nursing school graduate when it ended. In 1946 she secured a job at the Palmer Hospital and, at long last, was on her way to Alaska. For a year she put in her time at the hospital. A young and optimistic outdoors person, Charlotte made the most of her time in Palmer. When she wasn't working she was socializing, skiing or hiking. All year she looked forward to the Brooks Range backpacking trip her uncle had promised her. In the summer of 1947 she, her Uncle Jess Allen and his gold mining partner, Kenneth Harvey, set out on their adventure.

A Fairbanks pilot flew us to Wiseman and we started up the middle fork of the Koyukuk River. Uncle Jess showed me how to stow my gear in my sleeping bag, then put it on my wooden Trapper Nelson packboard, which is what all the old timers used. He taught me that at all times a back country camper must have a knife in his right pants pocket, matches in a waterproof container in his left pocket, and fishing line and a few hooks in his back pocket. That way, in case you went into the river, you could survive.

Uncle Jess and Harvey had a claim on Nolan Creek, along with several other miners. As we tromped through that country, all the men were working their claims. They invited me to dig down into the crevasses and get some gold, which I did. I got about an ounce.

148

I was 25 at the time. I had hiked a lot but never with a packboard, so that was a new thing. Also, the mosquitoes were fierce, and we didn't have any bug dope or headnets. I seem to recall that we had some 6-12, but that was all. We were really bushwhacking. I remember coming down off a ridge and when we got down to the gravel bar, away from the bushes, the two men quickly gathered dry driftwood and made a fire, to get rid of the mosquitoes.

They had two caches, one about 50 miles up the river, and one about 60 miles up. Their routine had always been to go upriver and get a moose or two, or a mountain sheep or two, maybe some caribou. They would then do the butchering and put the frozen meat on top of the cache. After the river glaciered up, they would come back with dog teams, bring it all back, and leave the next year's supply of food.

My backpack weighed about 30 pounds. Uncle Jess carried about 50 pounds and a 12-pound gun, and Harvey had 100 pounds. He was carrying a lot of extras: coffee, butter, bacon, etc., because they weren't sure there would be anything on the cache. They had taken the food up in '41 and, because of the war, hadn't been able to get back until our trip.

We climbed three miles up and over Hammond River Canyon. It was really rough going. There were no trails and it was quite steep. Harvey was ready to quit at the top but Uncle Jess just laughed at him, because there was no water up there. We had to keep going, all the way down the other side. It seemed like a very long way. My knees were really beginning to complain.

We were on a gravel bar off and on. We had to wade the river I don't know how many times. The first time, everybody took their boots and socks off and went across barefoot, and it was terrible. So the next time we took our socks off, took the insoles out of our boots, put the boots back on and crossed. Then we dumped out the water and put the insoles back in. That was a lot more bearable. Those rivers are terribly cold and the rocks are sharp.

At one point we saw a caribou running down the gravel bar; it practically ran through our camp. Harvey said, "Something's chasing it." I said, "Look, it's a fox." But it wasn't a fox; it was a wolf. There was a $30 bounty on wolves, so Harvey decided to save the caribou. He shot the wolf, skinned it, and saved the right foreleg, which you had to show in order to get the bounty.

We finally reached the first cache and put up our "permanent" camp. We were delighted to find that the cache was in fine shape. It was about nine feet off the ground, with a five-gallon gas can cut up and tacked around the pole, to keep animals from getting to it. It contained three 50-pound lard pails filled with oatmeal, rice, canned butter, coffee, pancake flour, a can of powdered eggs and a five-pound can of honey.

When we got settled in, Uncle Jess said, "Now it's time to go sheep hunting," meaning it was time for *me* to go sheep hunting. He had me sight in the rifle, and Harvey and I took off over the hillside. We hiked eight miles up a ridge and there was a sheep, sitting on a ledge, looking out at the universe. We couldn't shoot him because he'd have fallen off. So we hunkered down behind a hill and almost froze to death, waiting for the damn thing to move. When he did, I got him. I was pleased that I'd hit the sheep but felt a little pensive about killing something.

Harvey gutted it and we packed the liver, heart, tongue, kidneys and pancreas to take with us. Then Harvey piled some brush over the carcass and we hiked back to camp and had a wonderful liver dinner. I was hungry enough to eat a horse. The two men then hiked back for the rest of the meat.

Uncle Jess left me a gun, and told me to only shoot "unfriendly" bears. We were using a piece of airplane fabric for a tent, and bed nets. I was so tired, I crawled into the sack, tucking in my bed net, and I was gone. I wouldn't have cared if 14 bears had come.

They brought back the rest of the sheep on packboards, set up a tripod and started smoking it. Meanwhile we were lapping up wonderful sheep meat. It's the best meat I've ever eaten. It isn't even remotely similar to mutton.

We camped there for a week, then we put

Charlotte Allen Rogers on Ekok Creek, 50 miles north of Wiseman, 1949

the things we weren't going to take with us up on the cache, including the tripod of smoked meat, and hiked to the upper cache. There we caught quite a few grayling. We were eating high on the hog. Uncle Jess was always the cook; he was a wonderful cook. He was frequently aggravated at Harvey though because many times, when he got his fire just right, Harvey would come along with an arm load of wood and dump it on the fire.

One day Harvey and I hiked up to Ekok Mountain, where we could look down into the headwaters of the Chandalar River. I've always been interested in rivers. When we were kids in Williams River, West Virginia, one day we followed a creek clear to its headwaters, and it was just two or three little springs bubbling out of the ground. To me such things are fascinating!

We were gone almost exactly a month. When we got back to "civilization," I had a hard time sleeping that first night, closed in a cabin, rather than under the stars. Needless to say, it was an absolutely unforgettable trip. We returned to Fairbanks and I began working at the hospital as well as taking classes at UAF. In 1950 I married and had two children. When my marriage ended, I moved Outside to raise the children. Before settling down, we spent six months camping in Europe and eventually put down roots in San Jose, California. Each year I took my kids on extended backpacking trips on the John Muir Trail.

I was homesick for Alaska. In 1971, when my son and daughter were off to college, I immediately headed back. This time it was to Barrow, where I worked at the hospital for 15 years. I loved it there. The people were so wonderful. When I wasn't working I was always outside. I did a lot of skiing. I had a kayak. I had an 18-foot Klepper with a sail, which I used on the Beaufort Sea. Each summer I played softball for the Barrow Beauties, sponsored by Pepe's Mexican Restaurant.

Now I make it my business to do whatever I want to do, whenever possible. I do a lot of gardening. In the winter I ski two or three times a week. I go to Denali twice a year. In June I go for the flowers and in August I pick berries. I've done that for the last 15 years. Sometimes a friend or one of my grandchildren goes with me. Sometimes I go alone. It doesn't really matter. As long as I'm outdoors, I'm happy.

Marie "Teen" Cox Radtke

I was born in 1916 in Tecumseh, Nebraska. After high school, I attended St. Mary's College in Omaha, then St. Joseph's School of Nursing in Denver, Colorado. After nursing school, I continued at the hospital as a private nurse, sometimes working 12 hours a day, seven days a week. In the meantime I had gotten acquainted with Del Cox. He worked at the Texaco filling station near the hospital, where I always took my car to be serviced. One day he put my car (with me in it) up on the lift, and wouldn't let me down until I agreed to marry him. So I did. We ended up moving to Santa Monica, California, where he worked at Douglas Aircraft as a sheet metal specialist.

By that time, we had our first child, Gary. Thirteen months later Danny was born. All along, Del and I had talked about going to Alaska, but not really seriously. Then one day in July of '46, Del came home from work and announced that we were going to Alaska. He added, rather sheepishly, "Aren't we?" I said yes, but that we'd have to sell the house first. Ten days later it was sold. We drove to Seattle and boarded the steamship *Denali*.

We arrived in Seward and took the train to Anchorage. When we pulled into the station, a very nice cab driver let us know right away that we were going to have a hard time finding a room. He took us to the Westward, where they told us there were no rooms available.

The driver then took us to two more hotels, neither of which had any rooms. There didn't seem to be any alternative, so I told him to take us back to the Westward. The same clerk was on duty, but I didn't say a word to her, I just started moving furniture around in the lobby and turning out some of the lamps. When the clerk finally noticed us, she said, "What are you doing?" I said, "I'm certainly not going to walk the streets. I'm going to make my family as comfortable as I can." She said, "You can't do that." I said, "Sure I can. It's no problem." I wasn't at all surprised when, a little later, she came out and said, "We just so happen to have found a room."

Del got a job at Pacific Northern Airlines and, when our escrow money arrived, we bought a little one-bedroom place out in Spenard. Thirteen months later we moved to Skagway, where Del was hired to work on the railroad. Housing was scarce in Skagway too. We ended up renting a three-bedroom house that was so small, I called it the dog kennel. The place slanted so badly, if you went through the kitchen too fast, you'd smack right into the bedroom wall.

Eventually we ended up with a nice home, and we really enjoyed our 14 years in Skagway. While we were there I started the cub scouts; they'd never had a cub scout troop there before. I was tax assessor for several years, and I wrote for the *Juneau Empire Times* for a few years.

One day Del heard that a psychiatric hospital was going to be set up in Valdez. Until then, mentally ill people in Alaska had all been sent to a place called Morningside, in Portland, Oregon. Both of us put in applications and we both got hired. I was to be head nurse for the women's unit.

We arrived in Valdez in July of '61. In September everything was all set up. I flew down to Portland with an LPN, Mary Paine, and brought back 53 patients. They were either mentally retarded or handicapped or had some

Marie Radtke, fresh out of nursing school, 1938

kind of psychosis. It was quite a trip. They sent the head honcho from Portland, along with a couple of male aides, and we didn't have a single problem on the flight.

My son Danny was a senior in high school in 1964. In those days they let the seniors out of school to work the boats, so that's where he was on the morning of Good Friday. He came home that afternoon, very discouraged, because he and his buddies hadn't been hired. He had just walked in the door when the earthquake started.

Oh what a thing that was! Our place was completely destroyed. You could hear timbers breaking all over the place. Then the floor tile started coming up and the whole building twisted. Soon thereafter the tidal wave started coming in. We couldn't get out of the house, which turned out to be a good thing. When we finally were able to get the door open, a huge crevasse had opened up right outside the door. In the panic of the situation, I think that if we'd been able to get the door open, we'd have gone right into it.

Here's an ironic thing. I had ordered groceries from Gilson's, which they delivered just before the quake. When we finally got out of the house, we grabbed the box of food. If I'd planned it, I couldn't have done a better job, because it was full of juice, cookies, crackers, all sorts of finger foods, and a carton of cigarettes.

We got the garage door open enough that we could scurry out under it. On our way out, we grabbed all the boots and coats we could find, threw them in the back of our station wagon, and took off. Everyone in town was in shock. People were just wandering around, not knowing what to do. Danny was in his truck, offering rides to anyone. We were told to get out of town, the sooner the better. When we got to the weigh station, I told Del to turn around, that I had to get to the hospital.

It was a very frightening experience for everyone, but especially so for psychiatric patients. The building was destroyed, but we managed to get all the patients into one corner of the dining room, which had held up okay. We then brought in as many mattresses as we could and told everybody we were going to have a slumber party. "We're not going to take our shoes or clothes off," we told them, "We're just going to lay down on the mattresses. If you can't sleep and you want to get up, just let us know and we'll help you."

We found the eight-millimeter projector and one roll of the "Lassie" film, which we ran all night, trying to keep everyone occupied. In their confusion, the patients kept trying to run out the door. It was a long, hard night. The lights kept going on and off. We'd have a little bit of Lassie, then the projector would stop, then we'd get a little more of Lassie. The patients who couldn't sleep would come over to where we were set up, and we would reassure them. The next day at noon the air force came in and airlifted the patients out.

After that, we loaded all the medications into the back of the station wagon and put all the food we could scrounge into Danny's truck. We didn't know where we were going or how bad it was going to be, we just knew that we had to leave. We were in a caravan of five cars, with Danny in the lead, and a plan to meet at the school in Glennallen. By that time, I had been up so long, I was hallucinating. I drove off the road three times. Finally Danny stopped and said, "I can't take much more of this. Let's stop at Tonsina Lodge and go into Glennallen in the morning."

Naturally, the Tonsina Lodge was full, so they put us on the third floor, which was fine. It was dusty and dirty and cold, but we were glad to take it. The owners, Margaret and Bob Frasier, were completely overwhelmed, but everyone did what they could to help. Our friend Gert helped with the cooking. I quickly learned how to run a commercial laundry. The others were doing various things, babysitting and so forth.

To take our minds off our troubles, we watched "The Hunchback of Notre Dame." Nine-year-old David kept saying, "Mama I don't feel good." I told him, "That's all right honey, none of us do, but we're together and nobody's hurt." He kept saying he didn't feel good, and when I finally took a good look at him, I realized he had the mumps. So we were stuck at the lodge for three more weeks, long after the fellows had gone back to Valdez, to see what they could salvage.

We sent the kids off to family members in Nebraska, then came to Anchorage and stayed with some good friends. We bought one of the empty lots across the street from them, built a house, and moved into it in time to get the kids back to school that fall. Even though we lost our home, we considered ourselves lucky. Thirty-two people lost their lives on the docks in Valdez. I shudder every time I think of how close Danny came to being one of them.

Del Cox died in December, 1980. Several years later Marie married her old friend, Earl Radtke. The two are now living in Anchorage.

Glenn McLain

Glenn McLain was born in Jasper, Alabama in 1907. Like many men of the Depression era, he gravitated to Alaska with the Corps of Engineers during World War II. He claims his voyage to Alaska via the Inland Passage - along with 600 Army troops - was uneventful, except for the unpalatable food, crowded conditions and rough seas.

My brother-in-law and I traveled from Oklahoma City by train to Seattle. One night as we were sleeping, the pot-bellied stove exploded, sending soot all over everyone and everything in the car. It was an awful mess. In order to travel with the troops to Alaska, I told the army I was a photographer. What I didn't tell them was that I was an amateur photographer. We had a scare when the Japanese tried to bomb us, but we weren't too worried; they were pretty far away.

Coming from Oklahoma, I nearly froze to death that first winter. Every dime I could spare, I bought heavy clothes. In spite of that, I wanted to stay in Alaska. With all the experiences I was having, I was in hog heaven. My wife, Ruth, was a school teacher back in Oklahoma. When she came up to see me, she decided she liked it here too, and she got a teaching job right away. We had three daughters; two were married and the youngest came with us to Alaska.

After the war it seemed like everyone got interested in photography, so I figured opening a photo shop was a good idea. I worked for Stewart's Photo for a short while, then I started my own shop, on Fourth Avenue near D Street. When my business was at its best, I had two more stores: a space in Penney's and a store in Spenard. I sold cameras and took them in for repairs, and it was also an outlet for me to display my photographs.

Ruth and I both loved the outdoors and we always packed around a lot of photo equipment, in the hopes of getting good nature and wildlife shots. One time we camped out for nine days, waiting for the breakup of Lake George. It wasn't uncommon to see chunks of ice as big as a house floating down the river, and I wanted to be there at the crucial moment. When the ice finally broke, water came roaring down through there so fast, we were very glad we were on high ground.

Back in those days you didn't need a permit to go to McNeil River, so one time Ruth and I flew over there to photograph the bears. We saw some big timbers that had washed up on the shore, kind of tangled up, and decided to put up our tent there. I had heard an old tale - that a fire will keep bears away - so we kept a pretty good fire going. I'd just thrown some fresh logs on it, and Ruth and I went into the tent for the night. Pretty soon we heard a bear snuffling and the next thing we knew, he had tripped over our tent rope. I whispered to Ruth not to make a sound and we just sat there, frozen. After a while we looked out, and there was the bear, sitting by the fire. (I always told people he was warming his feet.) Eventually he got up and wandered away. He didn't give us any trouble.

Ruth and I counted 42 bears one afternoon. We were sitting up on a little ledge, watching them catch fish. I had the movie camera on a tripod and I got some really great footage. After a while Ruth decided to walk up a little hill and take a nap. We didn't realize we were near a bear trail until a bear suddenly appeared on the path with a fish in its mouth. The salmon was so big, it shook the bear's head back and forth. I dropped to my knees and focused the camera on the bear; he didn't even know I was there. When he got up close

Glenn McLain in Seward, 1956

157

to Ruth, he stopped and took a good look at her, but he was more interested in the salmon, and he kept going.

One time I was way up north, flying around, hoping to photograph polar bears. We finally spotted one moseying along, so the pilot landed and while I was getting set up, all of a sudden the bear charged me. He was so close, the pilot couldn't shoot him, for fear of hitting me. I took off my cap and started waving it at the bear for all I was worth, and finally he wandered away. Later I paced it off and calculated he was within 38 feet of me.

I was photographing moose once, up on a little ledge behind some trees. The trees were all leafed out, and I was looking through the camera, when a moose came along and filled up the entire lens. He just stood there and stared at me. People thought I was foolish, taking chances like that, but I accumulated a lot of good footage. I displayed my pictures in the store and they got a lot of attention.

Finally I had so many photos and movies, I started making copies and selling them. I spliced my best footage together and made a feature-length movie. For a few years there, every spring I'd put together a full-length 16-millimeter film and show it in the Sydney Lawrence Auditorium.

In those days you couldn't use a sound track, so I made a tape of appropriate music and narrated. I was real proud of those films. There were some awfully funny cutaways. Disney even bought parts of one film. We often had sellout crowds. The films would run for a couple weeks in Anchorage, then we'd take them to various other towns. We traveled quite a bit with our big movie, "Out There." We spent six weeks in Fairbanks and showed it all around the Kenai. I also did a weekly TV show for a while.

In March of '64 I was in my 4th Avenue store and the ground started shaking. It just kept getting worse and worse. I went outside to see if the McKay Building was going to fall. All the cars were shuffling back and forth; if they didn't have their brakes set they were rolling into each other. It was quite an experience, one you never forget. My store was in a long, concrete-block building, next to a vacant lot. It was damaged pretty much beyond repair.

Over a period of three years, McLain was to suffer several blows. Soon after the earthquake he had a heart attack that required a long recovery. Then Ruth got cancer, which eventually caused her death. To be closer to family, the McLains consolidated their two remaining shops into one and moved Outside.

McLain returned to Alaska in the spring of 1972. He became reacquainted with Ruth's old friend, Burdie Strait, who had worked as secretary to the Anchorage School Board in the 60s. She and Glenn were married in 1972. Six years later the McLains went back to Oklahoma, so Glenn could be near his aging mother. They didn't intend to stay for 20 years, and their return in 1998 was a blessing for old friends and family members.

At 94, Glenn's health is failing now. Burdie lovingly tends him and helps him recall the old days in Alaska. "Glenn lived to fish," she tells me. "He was a fantastic finish carpenter too. He was also a gardener. We had the most beautiful vegetable and flower garden in Spenard; tour buses used to stop all the time. We finally had to ask them not to, because they kept picking the flowers."

Glenn McLain is glad to be back in Alaska. Placidly rocking in his chair, he smiles at the memory of tourists snatching flowers, and the thousands of pictures he took, and fishing trips with old friends long ago.

Yvonne Krotke

I was born in Casper, Wyoming, and the very first thing I can recall was being in a tent. We lived in Lander, Wyoming, where my father was in the construction business. Sometime later we moved to Monte Vista, Colorado. My father and his brother then started their own construction business.

All went well until the Depression hit. Those were tough times; my father lost his business. Jobs were very scarce and we felt lucky when Dad found a job building a chicken coop for a dollar a day. I remember my mother sending me to the neighbor's house to borrow a teaspoon of baking soda or some other food item. The neighbors, in turn, often borrowed from us.

My father decided he would do some gold mining, and after that we ended up living in a number of different states, living in various mining camps. We were like Gypsies, moving from one place to another. Dad's interest in mining was inspired by his father's trip to Nome at the turn of the century. My grandfather did very well on his gold claim, and with the money he made he went Outside and bought several horses and mules. He then brought them back to Alaska and sold them at a great profit.

Dad and Mother came to Alaska in 1940. Of course at that time there was no housing available, so they lived for a while in a tent at the end of L Street, overlooking the bluff. The following year they built a house in the Spenard area. Dad did eventually go to Nome. He had invented a mining plant for placer mining, which he had built and shipped to Nome. The interesting thing about that is, when he filed his claims in Nome, it turned out he had filed on the very same ground that his father had mined in the late 1800s.

I met my husband at a church picnic in 1939. There happened to be a ball game going on in an adjacent field, and my girlfriend and I decided we'd like to watch it. In the process of climbing over a barbed wire fence, my slacks got caught in the wire and I ended up gazing into the blue eyes of the fellow who came to my rescue. His name was Walt Krotke. That was the beginning of our romance, and we were married a year later.

Soon after World War II started we moved from Reno to San Pedro and then Richmond, California, where we went to work, wanting to do our part for the war effort. I was an acetylene torch burner. My job was to burn out big steel plates which were used in building the hulls of hospital ships. Walt did engineering work on the ships. After about 10 months, I was homesick to see my parents and we made the decision to come to Alaska.

In the spring of 1942, Walt, our two-year-old son, Warren, and I boarded the old Alaska steamship *Aleutian*. We had some real rough waters out in the gulf and I

Yvonne Krotke at Lake Spenard, 1943

was so seasick I was wishing I could just die and get it over with. It was our anniversary during the voyage and my dear husband brought a box of chocolates into our cabin, thinking they were an appropriate gift. Just the sight of them made me sick. I always told Walt that was the closest I ever came to wanting a divorce.

Housing was very hard to find when we arrived in Anchorage, but we were lucky because we were able to stay with my folks at first. Alaska felt like the land of plenty, because we had gotten used to rationing in the States. There were a few things that seemed to be in short supply in Anchorage, but there was no shortage of food. One item you couldn't buy was a new automobile tire. We had acquired an old Chevy and when it got a flat, Walt patched the tube and put a Reader's Digest between the tube and the tire, where the nail had gone through. We drove on that for many, many miles.

My parents raised chickens to supplement their meat source and also had neighbors wanting to buy the eggs. My father had built a cinder block coop for the chickens; there were between 50 and 60 of them. My mother went out to feed them one morning and, lo and behold, the chickens all had the croup. They were all croaking, with bad chest colds. Mother came back to the house all upset. She said, "I think we're going to lose them!" She thought about it for a while, then she got out her big jar of Vicks Vaporub, rubbed every single chicken's breast and saved them all. She didn't lose a one.

Walt was finally able to start building our first home on Spenard Road. He just about had the house finished when his father passed away in Indiana, so he flew out for the funeral. When he came back he said, "We've lived up here long enough. Let's go back to Nevada." So we headed back to Reno and Walt found work as an electrician. When he brought home his first paycheck I said, "Where's the rest of it?" He said, "This is it." We had gotten quite spoiled with the wages in Alaska. As soon as we could - maybe two months later - we bought a Buick and a little trailer, loaded up all our household possessions and started up the Alcan. So we never did live in the house that Walt built. We sold it and were later told that it was Gwennie's first little restaurant on Spenard Road.

Walt was one of Alaska Airlines' first employees, working as an electrician on their Pilgrim aircraft. As time went by, and with additional training and schooling, he moved up through the ranks as Avionics Technician and worked on all the planes they're flying today.

My first job was at Pacific Airmotive out at Merrill Field, doing secretarial work.

I left that job and stayed at home for six months when our second child, Sandra, was born, but I wanted to work, so I found a job as secretary for the CAA (Civil Aeronautics Administration). From there I went to work for the Alaska State Employment Service and stayed with them for 25 years. I went from doing clerical work to employment interviewer to manager. It was a challenging job, and a lot of responsibility, with a staff of about 30 to 40 employees. The biggest reward was placing people on jobs that meant bread and butter on the table for them.

The Manpower office moved several times. In 1948, when I first started, it was located upstairs over the National Bank of Alaska on 6th Avenue. The jobs available at that time were mostly for construction workers, office workers of all kinds, nurses, and, in spring and summer, cannery workers. It was a big deal when recruitment started to fill jobs on the North Slope, working with the unions. It was really an exciting time.

When the '64 earthquake hit, the Employment Service was open 24 hours a day. There was so much damage to everything, the roads, buildings, docks; I had to have employees on duty around the clock. We put hundreds of people to work during that period, all kinds of people for all kinds of jobs.

After 25 years I was offered a job with the Department of Public Safety as supervisor of the records and licensing division. I worked there five years and retired. I figured 30 years was enough. Walt had retired a year earlier and we went traveling. We made a pledge to see as many national parks as we possibly could.

I lost Walt in '96. He and I had a lovely home on Campbell Lake, but it involved a lot of upkeep. In '98 I decided to sell it. I couldn't see any point in mowing lawns and shoveling snow, plus my children were concerned about me living alone in such a big house. So I moved to Chester Park and found that it suits me very well.

Now my sister and I are traveling companions. We've gone on numerous trips and plan hopefully to go on many more. I continue to do a lot of volunteer work. I've been an active member of the Soroptomist Club for almost 40 years. I have served on the Salvation Army board, and I'm still with the Salvation Army Auxiliary. I'm active in my church, and I've been involved with lots of different committees and organizations here in Anchorage throughout my working years.

As I look back I feel I have had a great life and still am. Best of all I have been blessed with a wonderful, loving and close relationship with my family, including three great-grandchildren.

Chuck Parsons

Chuck Parsons was born and raised in Pennsylvania. As a young man he joined the Air Force and trained to be an aircraft mechanic. After the Normandy invasion, he and his crew traveled all over Europe, repairing damaged airplanes. When the war ended, he returned home and worked for a year as the shop teacher at the local high school. When the principal asked him to stay another year, he was tempted. But he wanted to give Alaska a try, at least for a year. After that, he told the principal, he just might be back.

When I landed in Anchorage in the summer of 1947 I was flat broke. I worked at Elmendorf Air Depot for about a year as an aircraft mechanic, then I went to work on a survey crew. That summer the Kenai burned and Anchorage was often covered with smoke.

I had a friend, Frank Bettsinger; he and I had been on the same mobile crew in Europe during the war. He told me that if I ever made it to Alaska, to look around and see if it would be a good place for a taxidermy business. He was a farm boy from upstate New York. He and I had both taken correspondence courses in taxidermy.

So I let Frank know I thought it might be a pretty lucrative endeavor, and he came up in the middle of the summer. He told me, "There's one complication though, I'm bringing up a new wife." I didn't think that would be a problem. I was living on base and building a log cabin in Spenard. I figured they could live in that till they found quarters.

Frank and I set up our taxidermy shop in a tent there in Spenard and we put out

Aspiring taxidermists Frank Bettsinger and Chuck Parsons, 1947

our sign, and boy, we started getting business right away. In the fall we started getting heads and hides and everybody wanted a bear rug. We had a fleshing beam out in the yard and after work we'd be fleshing these bear hides. It started to go into winter and, meanwhile, Frank had gotten hired at the air depot. He and his wife were starting to get their feet on the ground financially, and this taxidermy business looked like it was really going to go.

We'd send all these bear hides Outside to a tanner and when we got them back we'd mount the heads; everybody wanted them open mouth. We'd put in artificial teeth and sew the borders on the rugs. One day Frank said, "I've got some bad news, my wife and I have to go back home or else get a divorce." I didn't even hesitate, I said, "Gee Frank, there's no problem, just let her go." I was serious. Of course, I'd never been married. He said, "It's not quite that simple." I said, "I don't see the holdup. Tell her to go. Buy her a ticket."

Well, they left and the bear hides started coming back from the tanner. I was mounting bear hides and sewing borders and I was just swamped. One guy had brought a grizzly bear hide in, it was a beautiful big hide. He wanted it made into a rug. He also brought the skull, which he wanted me to mount on a plaque. I recognized him; he had a reputation as a terrible barroom fighter. He was reputed to have bitten the nose off one guy. This was Spenard, which was a little place, where everybody knew everybody, and he was one guy you didn't want to mess with.

So I went out into the alley, built a fire and put this skull in a bucket of water. Every so often I'd go out and check on it, and it was boiling merrily away. I got doing something else and when I went to check on it, the fire had gone out and the skull was gone. Most of the water had boiled off and some dog had come by, reached in there and hauled the skull out.

By that time I had switched jobs and was working for Fish and Wildlife. We were having a coffee break in the hangar one day and I was telling these guys my dilemma, that I needed a bear skull. They all laughed; they were speculating on my demise, and finally one of 'em said, "We've got a locker down in cold storage and I know there's at least a couple of bear skulls. Tonight after work we'll go down and take a look."

So we went down and there was one pretty good-sized skull, not as big as the other, but I thought, boy that's my only chance. It was pretty clean, but I finished cleaning it up. I had a birch burl and I polished that up and mounted the skull; it really looked nice on that burl.

I had two half-grown Keeshond pups at the time. When the grizzly hide came back from the tanner, I pulled it over me and got on my hands and knees, growling and chasing those pups around the cabin, just clowning around. I backed 'em into a corner, which I never should have done, 'cause they were terrified. When they dashed out of the corner, one of 'em grabbed the bear's nose and almost ripped it off.

I panicked, and of course I had to repair it. If it was any other place, I could've hidden the stitches, but boy up in the nose ... you talk about a seamstress! I took the tiniest little black stitches. You had to look awful close to see them. When the rug was ready, I called up the guy and he came over. The whole time he was there I stood near the door. I was ready to run if I had to.

He looked the rug over real good. He kept telling me, "Gee, that's a nice job, that's a real nice job." Then he picked up the plaque and I could see a kind of a scowl come over his face. I thought, this is it. Then he said, "It looks a little small." I took a deep breath and said, "When you boil 'em to get the meat off, they always shrink." He twisted it around and looked and I was edging toward the door some more and finally he smiled, told me thanks and paid me. That was the end of the taxidermy business for me. When I got rid of the last bear hide that winter, I said, I'm out of this business.

Stan Fredrickson was the Fish and Wildlife agent who provided the bear skull. Stan was with Clarence Rhodes, Alaska's Fish and Wildlife Director, on a flight in the Brooks Range when they disappeared that summer. An extended, massive search was started which is probably still the longest, most extensive search ever conducted in Alaska. The crash site was finally found some 25 years later.

When I left Anchorage a few years later my wife and I homesteaded at Anchor Point and fished on Kalgin Island. Those early days in Alaska were some of the best times of my life.

Lone Janson

I was born in 1927 in Denver and grew up in Vancouver, Washington, during World War II. I always wanted to come to Alaska, so I worked out a deal with my mother: that as long as I graduated high school, she wouldn't object. I went to school and worked as a waitress, squirreling away my tips, always dreaming about going to the last frontier when the war was over. When that day came, I went straight to the steamship office and bought my ticket. I was so excited. I had just turned 18.

I landed in Skagway with $15 in my pocket and immediately started looking for work in a restaurant. Unfortunately, there was nothing available, but I heard about a job as a cook on the White Pass and Yukon Railroad. They must have been desperate, because they hired me, even though I told them I didn't know how to cook.

Riding that train was really a thrill. In some places it's two miles high, and you look down into an enormous canyon. Our destination was a little section house high above the canyon. Settling into my new job, I had no idea what to do with the frozen cow I found hanging in the freezer. But things turned out okay, and I merrily went on my way, cooking for five or six men, hacking off pieces of the cow when necessary. I was completely inept, but they were all very kind to me. I only stayed for about a month, until they could find a real cook. One of the highlights of my stay was seeing bears raiding the garbage cans and throwing them down the canyon.

I rode the train to Whitehorse and took the O'Hara Lines to Fairbanks - only the second civilian bus to travel the Alcan Highway after the war. It was the middle of winter when I arrived and there weren't a lot of jobs, but I was willing to do most anything. I washed dishes. I worked in a hotel. I worked in a laundry. I lived in the cheapest apartment I could find and did a lot of walking. I learned not to breathe through my mouth and to keep my glasses in my pocket until I got indoors. It was incredibly cold and the Northern Lights were amazingly beautiful.

I had begun hearing so much about Cordova, when spring rolled around, I decided I'd go there. The bus ride to Valdez took two days, and for the last leg of the trip I had to ride in a little two-seater airplane. The pilot had to piggy-back me out to his plane. He was someone I eventually came to know very well, Merle "Mudhole" Smith.

In Cordova I got a job on a floating cannery, which consisted of two scows, one for processing and one for storage. The ladies dorm, which had six or seven bunks, was on the processor. I grabbed an upper bunk with a window that looked out onto a beautiful waterfall. All the girls were so much fun; they were all young and single and full of hell. It was there we formed the "6:30 Club." Every morning a bunch of us would go swimming among the icebergs.

When the season ended and we got paid, I took a boat from Cordova to Seward, got on the train to Fairbanks, then flew to Nome. There I got a job waiting tables. I befriended a girl named Tony; she and I would go to the movies once a week. People hardly watched the movie, they were so busy throwing popcorn at each other. It was a regular popcorn war.

When winter set in I drifted down to Juneau with a friend named Julie. She got a job working for the governor's wife in their home. Knowing I had once worked in a laundry, she told them I was an experienced laundress, so they hired me too. My first night, they were having guests for dinner, and I was supposed to launder a lot of delicate, fancy things. I couldn't get them ironed in time, and oh it was a mess. Needless to say, I didn't work there long.

I hooked up with another friend, Angie, and we decided we'd go to Fairbanks. We couldn't find any work there, and I had received a note from the man who ran the floating cannery, asking if I wanted to work again, so Angie said, 'Let's hitchhike down to Cordova.' The first ride we got was in a truck with a man and his wife, which ended with the truck in a ditch. Angie and I were all right but the other two were unconscious. There we were, standing in the wilderness, wondering what to do next. A Native fellow found us and went for help a short way down the road. They got the car out and took us back to their place, where Angie and I entertained them with stories of our travels.

When we finally got to Valdez, we were weathered in for five days before Mudhole Smith could fly us to Cordova. While we waited, we worked in a little cafe; there was no bakery in town and Angie was a wonderful baker. People really hated to see her leave.

After that second fishing season, several of us worked for passage on a fishing boat going to Pelican City. We fished in Lituya Bay, which is quite remote and very historic. Lituya Bay is known for its history of natural disasters brought on by earthquakes and tidal waves.

When I returned to Cordova, I married Roy Hansen, who was born and raised in Katalla, across the Copper River flats. In the early 1900s, Katalla had been a prosperous settlement and first choice as the terminus of the Copper River and Northwestern Railroad connecting the Kennecott copper mines to tidewater. Because of its rich coal deposits, Katalla had once been known as the "Pittsburgh of the North." In the later 1940s it was considered a ghost town.

I had just turned 20, and living in a ghost town appealed to me. There were maybe three or four families living there, with a population of about 20. We spent the first winter of our marriage there. Here I could see evidence of the forgotten past in the old train engine abandoned in a field, old rails leading off into nothing. In Cordova I had walked the old railroad tracks and heard of the abandoned railroad. The seeds had been planted for my first book. From that time on, I sought out old-timers who told me about this part of Alaska's history.

Lone Janson on a floating fish cannery near Cordova, 1946

After that winter, we moved to Cordova, where we lived for the next few years and had two children. The marriage didn't last, though I remained in Cordova and later married Dick Janson, a very wonderful man, a lifelong Cordovan. He and I had a very happy marriage. We worked on a seine boat for 10 years in Prince William Sound. When Alaska got statehood, he became the first chairman of the Fish and Game Board. A Tlingit Native, Dick was an active participant in the Native corporations after ANCSA and became president of Chugach Alaska Native Corporation just before his death in 1977.

We lived in Cordova for 30 years. During those years, I was constantly writing on my book and had a weekly column in the local newspaper. As the new state came into its own, with oil development and a new awareness of Native rights, I began gathering historical information about Native issues. I started working for various statewide Native corporations as a historian. I was an editor for Alaska Native Management Report. When that was discontinued, I started my own version, Highlights of Native Business, publishing until its usefulness ended.

Over the years I wrote about Alaska for so many publications, it was impossible to keep count. I was in the right place at the right time, substituting for the Reuters correspondent in Alaska in the spring of 1964, and was able to wire some of the first news from Alaska to the South 48 in the aftermath of the Great Alaska Earthquake. In 1975 my first book, *The Copper Spike*, finally came out. It had only taken 25 years to complete!

My second book was in collaboration with my old friend Mudhole Smith. The book, called simply, *Mudhole Smith*, told the story of the airline he started in Cordova, later to become a major acquisition of Alaska Airlines. Good old Mudhole. He was dying as I was finishing his book. I was really racing against the clock, but I got it to him just in time. I think he was really pleased to know that his story wouldn't be forgotten. He was really a remarkable man.

I've just finalized a book about Jo King, a well-known female Alaska aviator. Another book I started a long time ago, about my early days in Alaska, is nearly completed. It seems like I've been writing ever since I learned to hold a pencil. I've had such fun over the years. I'll always be grateful that my mother encouraged me to come to Alaska.

Lorene Harrison

I was born on a farm in Kansas in 1905. I graduated from college in 1928 with a BA in home economics. My plan was to teach, but not in Kansas; I wanted to go to far away places. In my final year of college, we were given an assignment to write a term paper on a culture unfamiliar to us, so I chose the Alaskan Eskimo. I had a very hard time finding much about them in the library, and in my search I became more and more interested in Alaska. I could tell from the maps that there were only four towns of any size: Ketchikan, Juneau, Fairbanks and Anchorage. I did a very daring thing and sent my resume to all of them.

That summer I worked at Yellowstone National Park as an entertainer. While I was there I received a telegram saying I had been hired to teach music and home economics at the Anchorage Public School. I was to report for duty before August 26th. I was thrilled to death, but my folks were not. My mother's reaction was, *Alaska? Whoever heard of Alaska?* Fortunately, she knew of another girl from a nearby Kansas town who was also going to teach in Anchorage, Lois Lehman. So Mom hopped on the train, went to meet her, and decided that Lois was very nice. After that she figured it would probably be okay for me to come to Alaska; that there would be at least two nice girls up here.

When I fulfilled my commitment in Yellowstone, I took the train to Seattle to await the steamer *Yukon*. I met Lois the night before we left, and we got along famously, but I was always sorry that I didn't have a chance to tell my parents goodbye in person. We had a wonderful time on the boat. When it docked in Juneau, I noticed a young woman boarding, carrying a violin case. Her name at that time was Rica Niemi. She later married Frank Swanson. She had been working in the Palace

172

Theater in Juneau as part of the orchestra that accompanied the movies. She and I became fast friends and, seeing that there was a piano aboard the *Yukon*, the two of us entertained the other passengers. To this day we're still good friends.

When I got to Anchorage, it was love at first sight. Cook Inlet and the Chugach Mountains; I'd never seen so much beauty! A big yellow bus took us to the Anchorage Hotel, where we spent our first three nights. After that we moved into an apartment at the corner of 4th and G.

There was only one school in Anchorage, located where the Performing Arts Center is today. In addition to teaching music and home economics, I also had to teach several other subjects, including general science, which I had never studied. Nevertheless, I had a wonderful year. I was still young enough that the students felt they could talk to me, and I was included in most of their get-togethers.

I started dating Jack Harrison about a year after I arrived. On our second date he hired a World War I flying ace to take us up in a plane on the day of the summer solstice. That really caught my attention. At that point my father became quite ill,

Lorene Harrison entertains at the Anchorage USO, 1943

and I went back to Kansas to spend a year with my folks and to teach school in a nearby town. Jack came out to spend Christmas with me, and we were married the following July, on a mountain top near Denver. We were together 33 years.

Our first child, Pegge, was almost two when we returned to Alaska in early 1934. We had tried to make a go of it Outside, but the Depression hit us too hard. Jack's stepfather was living in Anchorage, and he loaned us the money to come back up. We were so happy to be going back to Alaska. We both knew we were going home.

Jack got a job as a fireman and then as an engineer on the railroad. I kept house, took in sewing and taught voice and piano lessons. We lived in a log house with Dad Sullivan and his two high-school age children, Doris and Charles. This was right downtown, near the school. Our second child, Carol Anne, was born in November, 1934.

We had such fun in those days. There was a group of people who were becoming, in some cases, lifelong friends. On Saturday nights Jack and I would go to the Elks Club and dance. One of the orchestras was the Meyers Family, four boys and their mother. She played the piano and the boys each played an instrument.

I became director of the First Presbyterian Church Choir and a few years later, during the war, I was music director and hostess for the USO (United Service Organization). It was the largest USO under the American flag. It was located at 5th and G, in a beautiful log building. Those were some of the happiest years of my life. The USO opened at seven in the morning and stayed open pretty much all night. In addition to all the other activities at the USO, we had community sings there on a regular basis, and there was always something special on Sunday evenings. We put on concerts and shows, celebrations of all kinds. It was so thrilling to me, to bring people together musically. Our girls were eight and 10 by that time, and they would come to the USO every day after school. The soldiers, who missed their own children, were so kind to them.

In 1944 my father had an attack of pneumonia and, since I was working for the government, I was allowed to go Outside. There were very strict rules in the military; the boys in the service couldn't tell their families where they were. But that rule didn't apply to me. It was perfectly fine, when I got to the States, for me to call their parents and tell them I'd seen their sons yesterday in Anchorage, Alaska. You can imagine what a thrill that was for the families. I must've made 50 calls. It always makes me happy to think of that.

In 1948 I opened The Hat Box. I had been making hats for quite some time, partly because I enjoyed it, but also because you couldn't find a decent hat in Anchorage, except caps for keeping your ears warm. By then all the military wives had returned to Anchorage, and they were very dressy. They wore hats and white gloves and carried purses, even to the grocery store. Right away The Hat Box became a real social place. I had to change location six times; the store kept getting larger and larger. It became the first bridal shop in Anchorage, with all kinds of luxury items, beautiful evening gowns and so forth.

I went on buying trips to New York every year for 20 years, sometimes twice a year. As luck would have it, one of the young soldiers I had befriended in Anchorage had become credit manager of the Waldorf Astoria Hotel and he made sure I was well taken care of. I always stayed in New York for two weeks. Not only would I buy hats and dresses, I saw all the Broadway shows. I was always making plans for how I could upscale our fashion shows in Alaska. When I'd return from my trip East, the women would just swarm to the store.

For an ordinary farm girl, I've had the most wonderful experiences. Coming to Alaska allowed me to do that. There was so much to be done here; it just seemed natural, to start doing it. At times, in the shop when all the women would be socializing, or during some musical event, I almost felt like I should pinch myself, to see if I was dreaming. I've lived a fairy tale life, and here I am at 97 years old, still going.

Lorene Harrison's story is huge. She directed the Presbyterian Church Choir for 27 years. She directed the Anchorage Community Chorus. She and a few key others started the Anchorage Little Theater. In the late 40s she had a radio show, and in 1950 became the first woman in Anchorage to have a TV show. In the 60s she became official chaperone for the Miss Alaska contestants at Atlantic City each year. Her awards, trophies and lists of achievements go on and on.

To her credit, Mrs. Harrison undertook the task of telling her life story, which necessarily includes the evolution of Anchorage, especially its culture scene. **Mostly Music**, *as told to and written by Dianne Barske, is widely available and guaranteed to make any reader marvel at how much one person can accomplish in a single lifetime.*

Vince Doran

84-year-old Vince Doran doesn't allow any grass to grow under his feet. He sleeps and takes meals at the Anchorage Pioneers Home, but he's out and about most of the time. A consultant to STEELFAB, he's constantly on the go.

A large map hangs on Vince's wall, nearly covered with flagged pins. Each pin represents a place he has visited. This summer he added flags to the villages of Atqasak and Nuiqsut. In 2002 he is scheduled to go to Kaktovik. All three communities are on the shores of the Arctic Ocean.

I was born in 1917 in Ephrata, Washington. I studied engineering at Gonzaga University in Spokane until I ran out of money, then I worked as a surveyor on construction jobs for several years. I was finishing work on an airfield in Spokane when a recruiter asked me if I'd be interested in working in Alaska. The pay was much better up here, so I came to Alaska in 1941, to the Sitka Naval Station. The next year the Civil Aviation Authority hired me to go out to the Naknek Army Air Base. At that point I was looking to get into the military. In Naknek I had many occasions to observe both the walking Army and the flying Army. There was quite a difference in the way they lived, so I figured I'd better get into the flying Army.

When the job in Naknek was over, I came back to Anchorage and tried to join the aviation cadets. Of course, everybody wanted to join the air corps, and everybody wanted to be a pilot. The recruiter told us that out of a thousand men applying for pilot training, only 39 would actually stay the course and get their wings. I said, "That's just about the right odds. Sign me up."

I've always been underweight, so the Army gave me seven days to get my weight up to minimum. I'd go into a restaurant and eat as much as I possibly could, but I could only gain a pound or two. Finally I went to see a fine old Anchorage doctor, Dr. Walkowski, and he told me I should eat a lot of bananas. The only thing was, there wasn't a banana to be had in all of Anchorage.

The recruiting office was out at Fort Richardson. When it was time for my exam, I drank two quarts of water, got in a cab and told the driver to get out there as fast as he could. On the way, I kept drinking more water. It was a slow going because the military police had decided to search cars, and by the time I got there I was ready to burst.

Before they put me on the scale they had me undress and lay on the exam table. My stomach was distended from the water, causing a bulge, and when the doctor poked me there, I let out a howl. When I told him what the story was, he called the other doctor over, and they both had a good laugh about it. Then he wrote the minimum weight on my chart, and I was in the Army Air Corps.

I went to several military flying schools and I did get my wings. I became a pilot and a commissioned officer. I took more training and was sent to the Eighth Air Force in England. From there I bombed the hell out of Germany 33 times.

When the war ended I went back to college in Spokane, but I was restless. The last thing I wanted was to be in school. When I learned it would take an extra year to get my engineering degree, I switched majors and got my degree in philosophy. I only wanted to graduate.

Vince Doran surveying near Sitka, 1941

I wanted to stay in aviation, but I didn't want to fly for an airlines, so I ran a little flying service at Coulee Dam for a couple years. In the meantime I met a fine young lady in Spokane, a nurse, Jean Birrer. We were married in 1949.

I had signed up for five years in the Air Force reserves and in 1949 was called back in, at the time of the Berlin airlift. I was sent to a base in Tripoli, Libya, where I worked for a year. My primary duty was new construction and base maintenance, and my secondary duty was flying.

When I returned to Washington state, I did construction work for Morrison-Knutsen for several years, both there and in Alaska. When I went to Alaska our son, Vince Jr., was two years old and our second child was on the way. Jean went to stay with her mother in Missoula and when I went to visit them, my son didn't even know me. I couldn't handle that. I wanted to be with my family.

My next job was to have been in French Morocco. I'd have loved to have had my family there. The kids could have learned French; we'd have had a great time. But no one was allowed to bring their families in those days. So I decided to stay in Alaska. My family joined me here, and we all settled in.

Construction took me all over Alaska. In the 50s I was involved with the construction of a radar station on St. Lawrence Island. When we got there it was just barren ground. We built roads, runways, power plants, buildings, everything. Working on the White Alice project also allowed me to travel all over Alaska. White Alice was a code word for a military communications system used during the Cold War. The last job I had was maintaining communications in 33 stations, an area covering a quarter of a million square miles.

In 1964 Al Swalling hired me to manage Steel Fabricators, a structural steel fabricating and supply business. I've been there ever since. In 1970, when the Alyeska Pipeline construction started, camps needed sewage treatment plants. I designed a portable, packaged plant and had it tested by the National Sanitation Foundation at their laboratory in Ann Arbor, Michigan. It tested well, and we have been manufacturing them ever since. We have just finished plants for all seven of the North Slope Borough's villages.

Al sold the business to Janet and Richard Faulkner, who changed the name to STEELFAB. I retired, but Richard asked me to stay as part-time consultant. I eagerly agreed because I need to be useful, and my heart wasn't in retirement.
I have other interests. I put out a monthly newsletter for the Pioneer Home. I'm a

Toastmaster. I give entertaining speeches and humorous speeches. Sometimes I recite poetry. I speak wherever anyone will listen to me. I need intellectual stimulation, and I need to keep busy. I've just returned from a trip to the "High Arctic," as the people there term it. An old friend of mine, Paul Crews, called me and said he was going on an expedition to the north magnetic pole and asked if I'd like to join him. I couldn't think of any reason why not.

We flew from Anchorage to Ottawa, where we joined the rest of our group, which consisted of 86 people from 15 different countries. Most were European, and the group was pretty evenly split, men and women. We all got on a chartered plane and flew to the little town of Resolute on Cornwallis Island, in the far north of Canada. (Barrow is 71 degrees north; Resolute is 75 degrees north.)

There we got on a Russian icebreaker and for two weeks toured that part of the world, all around northeastern Canada and the northern tip of Greenland. We saw polar bear, musk ox, fox, and millions of birds. We were in all kinds of conditions: clear water, ice we could get through easily, ice we got through with difficulty, and ice we couldn't get through at all.

We went ashore every morning and afternoon, either by inflatable boat or helicopter. If there was no ice along the shore edge we'd go by Zodiak. We'd walk around the country and see the flora and fauna. At the end of the day there were always lively discussions. Sometimes there would be a slide show or lecture.

On one trip ashore on Beechy Island, we saw grave markers of three men who had been on Franklin's ill-fated expedition in the early 1800s. We got as far north as 81 degrees on Ellsmere Island, Canada's northernmost possession, about 500 miles from the North Pole. That expedition was the trip of a lifetime for me.

Margret Pate

Margret Pate is a very young 90-year-old. She annually travels to places like Malta and Peru and Uzbekistan. She gardens, bowls, luncheons regularly with her gal pals and speaks matter-of-factly about what it was like to be a newcomer to Alaska nearly 60 years ago.

My family, of course, thought I'd completely lost my mind. I sort of felt I had, too. It seemed like a wildly reckless thing to do. I was a third generation Oregonian who, like my mother and grandmother before me, had rarely been more than a hundred miles from home.

I was working for the Department of the Interior, working specifically in the legal department of the Bonneville Power Administration in Portland. One day in June of 1942 a young man from Anchorage showed up in my office. He said (referring to my co-worker and friend, Kathleen) "I desperately need legal secretaries in Alaska. Kathleen is willing to go if you are."

Kathleen was a very feminine, dainty city person. I thought, if she can dare to go to Alaska, I guess I can too. So I said, "Well, all right." Later I learned he had gone to Kathleen's office and told her that I was the one willing to go. She too said all right. Our personnel man insisted that our jobs were frozen. He kept saying, "These girls can't go!" But the recruiter told him we were on a war appointment and we'd be on the first available transport to Fort Richardson. And away we went.

We left Oregon on an Army "flying boxcar" filled with Jeeps, GIs and new recruits ranging from construction workers to military officers. It took us eight hours to fly from Portland to Anchorage, in bucket seats. I had never been in an airplane before, and we were quite uncomfortable.

We arrived safely and went blundering around Anchorage, trying to adjust to the continual daylight, to the delight of those who had already been in Alaska for a week or so. The city itself was an eye-opener. 4th Avenue was paved only a few blocks. There was nothing much on 5th Avenue. There were lots of cabins scattered around on trails, and homes on unimproved roads. There was nothing in the Spenard area. Other than the military comings and goings at the base at Fort Richardson, the bars seemed to be the main activity in town, with a surprising number of nice shops.

I soon became familiar with small airplanes, hopping regularly to places like Seward, Fairbanks and Nome. On our first trip to Fairbanks, we happened to be in one of the forbidding passes in the mountains when the motor sputtered and appeared to be about to quit. The passenger in the seat in front of us, who could not have missed the fact that we were very new to Alaska, turned around and said quickly, "Put your foreheads on your hands, on the back of the seat in front of you. That way your neck will be broken when we crash and you won't suffer." Of course by the time he had given us these grisly instructions, the pilot switched to the full tank, and we proceeded safely into Fairbanks.

I met John Pate in Anchorage during the war. We married and moved to Homer in 1952. John was a very hirable person. He would do anything, it didn't matter if it was digging a ditch or driving a truck. Much to my relief, good child care was easy to find, and I went to work for Terminal Oil Sales.

Margret Pate in Anchorage, 1945

Eventually I became a licensed independent insurance agent and put in a year in the U.S. Commissioner's Office. That was strange and wonderful, to say the least. The position didn't have any salary attached to it; the only money you made were filings that you might do. Vital statistics were a part of the office, deeds of conveyance of property, that type of thing. Occasionally it was scary because you were the judge in certain capacities: probate judge, juvenile judge, coroner, and lots of things in between.

I was astonished to have John come in one night and ask me what I would think about homesteading. He had found a parcel of land that he really liked, right on the Anchor River. My folks had homesteaded in Oregon and I knew Mother hadn't particularly enjoyed that experience, but I agreed to give it a try. It turned out that that year John's job took him away from home a goodly portion of the time, and the children and I put in the seven months necessary to prove up on the land. We also had to accomplish a stipulated amount of cultivation.

The cabin was three-quarters of a mile off the Old Sterling Highway, through brush and swamp, and for some reason I was terrified that the children and I would be eaten by bears. John warned me to be sure we got off the trail and did not challenge any moose, but somehow bears remained my problem. I kept looking at the scrubby trees, wondering if there were any large enough for me to get the children up, and then myself, before a bear got us. If so inclined, I am sure it would have taken a pretty slow bear not to get us. John was home on weekends and everything worked out quite smoothly. We got our homesteading adventure in, but we soon bought a lot and built a home in Homer.

In the early days in Homer, scheduled recreation for children was not a priority. School activities included basketball and track for boys, and nothing for girls. Family-wise, the children and I spent time at the beach. We swam in Beluga Lake until the leeches took over. We also swam out at Miller's Landing and Green Timbers, on the spit.

I'm still very happy that John made the decision that he wanted the kids to go to school here in Homer, in an area where nobody cared whether their dad was the garage man or the banker. He wanted simple, uncomplicated schooling for them. I used to worry a little bit about the lack of sophistication, but that didn't seem to be a real problem.

In the spring of 2001, Mrs. Pate traveled to the Basque Country in northwestern Spain and to southwestern France. In the fall she visited China.

Charles Sappah

The oldest living ex-FBI employee in Alaska, Charles Sappah looks much younger than his 83 years. He and his wife, Marge, invite me into their home, supply me with freshly brewed coffee, and we chat about the unique circumstances that brought Mr. Sappah to Alaska.

Both the Sappahs are certified ham radio operators and, when we begin looking through their photo albums, I am stunned and delighted to discover that beneath the pictures of their radio friends are what appear to be license plate numbers rather than names. This makes perfect sense, of course, and the Sappahs are pleased that I am so easily amused.

I was born on Armistice Day, November 11, 1918 in Jersey City. When I graduated from high school I started looking for work in New York City. I went to various places, a bank, among them, and I thought, gee I'd have to dress up and wear a hat and all that; that's really not my style. Then I walked past an armory where civil service jobs were posted. One of them was for the fingerprint department of the FBI. That sounded a lot more interesting than working in a bank. It turned out they were giving tests that very day. I passed the test, then pretty much forgot all about it. In early 1941 I got a telegram from the FBI, wondering if I was still interested in the job. Absolutely!

I spent a year and a half in Washington D.C., learning all about finger printing. During that time the bureau decided they wanted to start a radio section. Radio had been an interest of mine since I was 12 years old, so I went into that. From 1943 until 1944 I was assigned to Juneau, as a ham radio operator. Four of us ran the radio station there. I was a big city boy who'd never really been out of the city,

and I loved the feeling of camaraderie we had; we were a real close-knit group. We used to get together at Mike's Place, a homey kind of bar where they fed you family style and served steak.

I was transferred to Anchorage in 1944. Two men came up from Washington, D.C., plus the three or four of us who had been assigned there, and we put the radio station together, in a Quonset hut out on Fireweed Lane and Blueberry Road. It was a nice big old Quonset hut, on two or three acres of land. We handled lots of traffic. During the war we were always monitoring the Japanese stations, listening to their conversations and so forth. Their transmissions were all in five-letter code groups that we copied and sent to Washington. We had no idea what they contained.

The bureau had a command car, a big Army car with huge wheels, which I drove to work. Of course, practically nothing was paved in Anchorage at that time. In the spring, the ruts would freeze and thaw, and you really had to make sure you were in the right ruts when you were going up Romig Hill, in order to make the left hand turn onto Fireweed. I often towed people out of the ditches with that big old eight-cylinder Dodge. It really had a lot of power.

All in all, things were pretty quiet up here during the war. The Japanese sent hun-

Charles Sappah leans against the FBI's "big old eight-cylinder Dodge" in Anchorage, 1944

dreds of balloons with incendiary devices to the West Coast, a few of which landed in Alaska. They didn't do any damage though, because they landed out on the tundra. Several of them landed in Oregon, however, and started small forest fires.

I met my wife, Marge, in Washington D.C. while I was receiving some additional training. She also worked for the FBI, as a typist. I was to be posted in Nicaragua for three months, for the purpose of closing down the station there, and Marge and I agreed to marry when I returned. When three months came and went and still the station hadn't closed, we decided to marry in Nicaragua. I ended up spending 18 months there; Marge returned to the States several months earlier. In fact, I got back just in time for the birth of our first child in New Jersey. I was really hoping for the opportunity to return to Alaska and, sure enough, in 1947 a job became available and we moved to Anchorage.

We lived in one of the three barracks buildings on 13th and I. It was a great place to raise kids; everyone knew everyone and it was close to town. The buildings were practically a whole block long. If you piled snow around the edges of the building, the fire department would flood it for you, making it a skating rink. We lived in that place for five years. That's where Marge and I got our ham tickets; we've both been ham radio operators for over 50 years.

After five years in the barracks building, I got transferred back to Washington D.C. in 1952. I hated to leave Alaska, so I told Hirsch Frickey, the fellow who had Yukon Radio Supply on 7th and I, that if he ever decided to hire someone he should let me know. A year later a telegram arrived, letting me know the job was available.

It was a sad day for me, resigning from the FBI after 14 years. I had really enjoyed working for them; the espirit de corps had always been so great. In the old days, my office had been right across the hall from J. Edgar Hoover, so I saw him frequently. When I turned in my credentials, I knew I could never walk through those doors again.

Probably the most interesting thing that happened while I worked for the FBI was an incident from the late 40s. There had to be somebody on duty 24 hours a day, so all of us took a night shift now and then. I was on duty; it was a Saturday night, and a man rapped on the door around 11 at night. When I answered, he said, "I'd like to give myself up." I said, "What are you wanted for?" He said, "Bank robbery and murder."

185

I wasn't an agent and I didn't have a gun, so of course I was a little nervous. I told him to come in, and I got him settled in the clerk's office. Then I went into our file, and couldn't find a thing on him, so I called my boss in Chicago and told him the story. He said, "Put him in jail for the night and tomorrow morning we'll take care of it." I called the U.S. Marshall, who came over and put the man in the federal jail.

The next morning my boss called and, sure enough, this guy and a couple of his buddies had robbed a Brinks armored car. The only trouble was, they got practically no money, just non-negotiable bonds, and a thousand dollars, plus they killed the driver. So this guy took off for Seattle and used his share of the money to come to Alaska, thinking it would be a good place to hide. But when he got up here, he had no place to go and, without much money, he figured the best thing to do was to give himself up. The Bureau brought him back to Chicago, where he was subsequently convicted and sentenced to life in prison. That was sort of my crowning achievement with the FBI.

In 1953 I cut my ties with the FBI and we moved back to Alaska. In those days there weren't a lot of things for kids to do in Anchorage, but one of the things the kids really enjoyed was riding the city bus. There were so many chuck holes on the roads, our little girl would bounce almost to the ceiling of the bus. She thought that was the greatest thing in the world.

I worked at Yukon Radio Supply in Anchorage for 25 years. For two of those years we were in Valdez, and I ran the store there. Then in 1980 Yukon Radio closed their doors, so Harry Lang and I decided to start our own electronics shop, which we called Alaska Electronics. I was only in that for six years, retiring in 1987.

I'm still active in radio. I've belonged to a ham radio club in England for 20 years. I use code - all dits and dots - and I get responses from people all over the world. It's very interesting, shooting the breeze with people, most of whom I've met, but many that I haven't. Lots of times I'll be talking with someone and another person will join the conversation. Sometimes there are as many as four of us.

I still keep in touch with the radio communicators from the bureau, and Marge and I play a lot of duplicate bridge. We have three children, 11 grandchildren and seven great-grandchildren, all living here in Alaska. Between keeping up with my family and playing around with the radio, life is pretty full.

Jack Lentfer

Jack Lentfer is one busy guy. As I'm being ushered into his Homer office, another guest is just leaving. We only have an hour to talk because Jack and his wife, Mary, will soon be heading to Anchorage, where he's scheduled to publicly read an article he's recently written. His writings, like his life, revolve around the recurring theme of wildlife.

Lentfer has twice been president of Alaska's chapter of the Wildlife Society. In 1991 he received a presidential appointment to serve on the U.S. Marine Mammal Commission. He has also served on the Alaska Board of Game. Over the years he has published dozens of articles pertaining to conservation and wildlife.

I was born in Livingston, Montana in 1931. My first serious thought about Alaska was when I was in seventh grade. Life magazine had a spread on a homesteader and his wife who lived at the mouth of the Colville, on the Arctic coast. I remember thinking that I'd sure like to get up there.

After college and two years in the army, I went to work for Montana Fish and Game. Pretty soon an opportunity with the Fish and Wildlife Service in Alaska came along, and I didn't even hesitate. In June of 1957 I loaded everything I owned into a little Studebaker and drove up the Alcan Highway.

Alaska was a great place for a young biologist. When I was in Anchorage I slept in a warehouse, but mostly I worked in the field. My first day on the job I flew down to Homer with a fisheries biologist and planted rainbow trout in China Poot Lake. I was with the Office of River Basin Studies, and we were concerned with federal water development projects and their effects on fish and wildlife. Wherever dams

187

Jack Lentfer on a Dall sheep hunt in the Chugach Mountains, 1964

were proposed, we would inventory the fish and wildlife resources and report on effects of development.

That first summer, four of us took a riverboat from Fairbanks down the Tanana River to the mouth of the lower Yukon. We were inventorying fish on fish camp drying racks and seining small fish for later identification. We had quite an adventure near the mouth of the Yukon. We got in a big headwind, took on a lot of water, and our boat swamped and turned over. I managed to climb up on the boat and the other three drifted downstream faster than I did. The river was wide and we eventually passed an Eskimo fish camp. I got their attention by hollering and they came out and picked us up.

I also spent time at a proposed dam site above Devil's Canyon, on the Susitna River. Later that fall I worked on proposed dam sites in the Copper River drainage. The Bradley Lake project, just outside of Homer, was also on the books. In 1958 another biologist and I took an old wooden skiff from Kenai to the head of Kachemak Bay and spent a week inventorying fish and wildlife to determine effects of a hydroelectric project.

Another big project was the Yukon River Rampart Dam proposal, which would have blocked salmon runs, flooded one of the most important waterfowl nesting areas in North America, and created a lake bigger than Lake Erie.

I met my wife, Mary, at a New Year's Eve party. She had worked as a nurse in Kotzebue and recently moved to Anchorage. We married and had three wonderful children. After statehood I worked for state Fish and Game and eventually started studying polar bears. This lead to a family move to Barrow in 1969 for three years. Barrow was a small community then, before the Native Claims Settlement Act and the pipeline, and we enjoyed it immensely. Mary worked as a nurse and we had hospital quarters in the village. I had my office at the Arctic Research Lab about four miles away. The kids stayed with a wonderful babysitter who taught them more Inupiat than I knew.

My most memorable trips were traveling by snowmachine and camping with Benny Ahmaogak, a polar bear hunter from Wainwright, to determine the feasibility of guided hunting for polar bears from the ground to replace hunting from airplanes. Polar bear studies really got started in the mid-60s after Bob Bartlett, the Alaska senator, convened a meeting at the university in Fairbanks of the five polar bear nations. Countries agreed to do research and share information. A polar bear specialists' group was formed and we met every two years in Switzerland, a neutral country where Soviets would send representatives during the Cold War. One of the first things we wanted to address was whether we had one circumpolar bear population, or whether there were several discrete (isolated) populations.

We started marking and recapturing bears, and learned that there were discrete populations. This then made each country responsible for management of bears that occurred offshore from its coast. Bears move around a lot, but when it's time to den, they seem to come back to the same general areas each year. Somehow they can navigate on moving ice and get to where they want to be.

One of our first major projects was to capture, mark and then recapture bears. We followed their tracks on the sea ice and then shot them with an immobilizing drug from a helicopter. We marked them, took weights and measurements, recorded data on reproductive status, and pulled a small tooth for age determination. The first time out, we were pretty cautious. The tranquilizing drug we were using hadn't really been tested, so we didn't know exactly what to expect. We were very much aware that there weren't any trees to climb.

I only had one close call with a bear. We had been following a female with a yearling cub for a long time through rough ice on a very cold day. When I finally shot

189

her, nothing happened, so I gave her another small dose, which was standard procedure. She went down with the second shot but it turned out that was only because she was tired from all the running around.

I walked up to immobilize the cub from the ground; Lee Miller, with whom I was working, was busy in the helicopter. When I was about 40 feet from the bear, she got up and started chasing me. The drug in the first syringe had frozen and was totally ineffective. By that time Lee was out of the helicopter and, sadly enough, he was forced to shoot the bear, which was about three feet behind me at that point.

I did field work for 12 years on polar bears. In 1972 we moved to Juneau, where I worked as a regional supervisor with more office work and less field work than before. The biggest issue we dealt with was studying the effects of logging on wildlife - mainly deer, mountain goats and some bears - in the Tongass Forest. What we learned is that clear-cutting and logging of old growth forest is indeed detrimental to wildlife populations.

After southeast Alaska, Mary and I moved to Homer, in 1987. One of the things that drew us back is our cabin and salt-water activities at Bear Cove, at the head of Kachemak Bay. I had staked five acres on open-to-entry land in 1970. We spent family vacations there and built a cabin from trees cut on the site. Our kids helped with peeling, notching, getting the logs up, and retrieving boats and gear carried away by the tide. We all have good memories of those times. Beetle-killed trees provided logs for a sauna we built a couple of years ago.

I also stay involved with habitat issues. I am particularly concerned now because of threats to polar bears and caribou from oil development on the Arctic National Wildlife Refuge. The refuge provides winter maternity denning habitat for more polar bears than any other land area in Alaska. Development activities could cause some bears to abandon dens and not produce, or lose their cubs. This could be critical to the population, which has a naturally low reproductive rate.

The coastal area of the refuge is also used by bears during the fall for feeding, resting and moving about. This use has increased in recent years and may be related to development activities to the west of the refuge. Global warming is causing sea ice to become thinner and could reduce the amount and quality of pack ice suitable for denning. This makes protection of quality denning habitat on the Arctic refuge even more important.

Caribou are another issue. The coastal plain of the Arctic refuge, where drilling is proposed, is the main calving area for the Porcupine caribou herd. The coastal plain is narrow, about 15 to 40 miles wide, so caribou that were displaced by drilling activity would have no place to move to. This is in contrast to the Prudhoe Bay area, where displaced caribou have a coastal plain that is 150 miles wide to move about in.

The amount of oil that might be available from the Arctic refuge does not justify the threats that development poses to wildlife. The refuge should remain what it was intended for - a refuge.

Harriet Hansen

Art and Harriet Hansen were living in Detroit when, in 1948, Art decided to rejoin the Army. He requested duty in Alaska and was soon on his way to Anchorage. Harriet owned a thriving beauty shop in Detroit and the thought of moving to Alaska didn't appeal to her in the least.

Harriet wearing a sealskin coat, early 50s

I was perfectly happy right where I was; I wasn't at all excited about Art going off to Alaska. I came up to visit him in 1949, thinking I was only going to stay a short while. But after I got up here, I discovered that I loved it. It was like nothing I'd ever seen. I went back to Detroit, closed my shop, and came back to Anchorage as soon as I could.

I had a lot to learn about Alaska when I first moved here. Being from the city and having had my own shop, I thought I knew it all. I figured the other women in the beauty business were absolutely waiting for me to arrive, so I could show them all how. To my surprise, I ran into stiffer competition in Alaska that I ever had in my life.

I went to work for Agnes Burns at the Westward Beauty Salon when the hotel was only seven stories tall. One of the local beauticians, Hester, had spent quite a bit of time in Guam; another woman, Pearl, had worked in a beauty salon in Paris. They were all so interesting and so much fun. You met so many characters back in those days. Anchorage was a very closely knit community, and in our line of work we were especially close. If Lois's shop couldn't take someone, they'd call Agnes's shop, or Maxine's shop; we all worked together. It was such fun.

It was soon after I got here that a Mother of Pearl cloud was visible, and I'm telling you, that was really something to see. It was in January of 1950; Art and I were living out in Fairview. I was walking to the grocery and a man on the street turned to me and said, "Look up at the sky! You'll never see that again!" The sky that day was a beautiful deep blue and when I looked up, there was a stratus cloud that contained every color of the rainbow, surrounded by a silvery sheen. It hovered in the sky from 11:00 in the morning until it got dark, at about 3:00. Art was working out at the base, and it was such a sensation, they let all the men off. Everyone was out taking pictures. I was told later it's a phenomenon that only happens close to the pole, and only about once in a century.

I was working at the old Cinderella Beauty Shop on 4th and D when Mt. Spurr erupted. Art dropped me off at the shop at about 8:00 in the morning, and when I looked across the inlet, I saw an unusual cone shape. I thought maybe it was a cyclone, so I called the radio station and was told, "You'll be in total darkness by 11:00." Sure enough, at five minutes to 11:00, everything was black. We watched out the window as people tried to walk. They couldn't really keep their eyes open fully, the ash was so heavy. In the middle of the afternoon it finally stopped, the sky turned a pretty blue, and there was all that awful black dirt on everything. The hangers-on at the old Union Club were all out, collecting ash to sell to the tourists.

There were only about 16 of us in the hairdressing business, but we wanted to become members of the National Hairdressers and Cosmetologists Association. We decided to recruit the hairdressers from Fairbanks, so we got a group of girls together and took the train up there. We had to go straight from work, so the train ride was our only chance to get dolled up. When we arrived in Fairbanks we had rollers and pin curls in our hair, and we were expected to attend a cocktail party where everyone was dressed to the nines.

As I recall, it was about 25 below, and we had a young girl from Florida; she hadn't been in Alaska long and she was dressed semi-formally, with a little fur jacket. She looked great, but she kept saying, "It's so cold! It's so cold!" The rest of us were all bundled up. We had a ball in Fairbanks. They put on a show like you wouldn't believe.

After working for Agnes for quite some time, I opened my own shop out in Spenard, Harriet's Magic Mirror. It was just a little tiny shop on skids, with no foundation. During the '64 earthquake, my entire cupboard of shampoos, permanent waves and solutions fell over. They were all in bottles, of course, so they all broke. The next day my son hosed out the place and I thought the suds would never stop washing out that door.

Back in the early days, I used to occasionally take the train up to Talkeetna with a girlfriend. It was always a fun and friendly place to visit. When I retired in 1976, I thought of going there to live, because it reminded me of Anchorage in the territory days. I bought a house there and Talkeetna welcomed me with open arms. I was so happy in my house by the Susitna River. I had a three-wheel bicycle; I used to cruise all around town. I had never learned to drive a car, but I could ride that bike.

One day I was talking to Dorothy Jones. I told her, "You know, I see kids coming down Ski Hill all the time and they look like they're having such fun; I'd like to do that too." She said something on the order of, "Go for it!" I told her, "The only problem is, I can't pedal all the way up there." She said, "Do what the kids do - push the bike up." She didn't seem to think that just because I was 70 years old, that should be a problem.

I pedaled as far as I could, then I pushed the bike the rest of the way up the hill. When I got to the top, I got on, let go of the brake, and I'm telling you, I came down that hill so fast, I was completely out of control. I've never been so scared, before or since. Poor old Orville Engelhorn, he just happened to be driving by; he was so worried when he saw me, he pulled off the road to see what was going to happen. I think he thought he might have to pick up the pieces. My jacket was flying out and my hair was blowing all over the place. I was afraid to put on the brake because I thought it might throw me. But finally the bike slowed down and I rode back to town just as though nothing had happened. No more than four people saw me on the hill, but when I got back to Dorothy's, everyone remarked, "You came down that hill pretty darn fast, Harriet."

When I first moved to Talkeetna, the *Anchorage Daily News* came up in the mail, so it was always a day late. I decided maybe a paper route would be a good idea. The people at the paper asked me, could I get 50 subscribers? I said, "That's an awful lot. How about 10?" He said okay. The paper would arrive on the train at 10:00, I'd pick it up on my bike, and deliver to various people. I kept that route for about a year, until eventually there were too many customers. I couldn't handle it anymore.

This summer I'll be getting around on my battery-powered wheelchair; it goes eight miles an hour. It has real thick tires, made for the outdoors. I got it last summer. I was just getting used to driving it down the alleys when the weather got cold.

Harriet served several terms as president of the Alaska chapter of National Hairdressers and Cosmetologists Association and received its leadership award in the mid-60s. When living full-time in Talkeetna became too difficult, Harriet returned to Anchorage. Just as soon as spring arrives, though, she heads back up the highway to her home on the river. Two of her three children now live in Talkeetna, as well as nine grandchildren.

Pointing with pride at her new chair, Harriet assures me she'll be back in Talkeetna soon. If you get up that way, keep an eye open for her; she's the lady with snow white hair, a perennial smile and the spirit of old-time Alaska.

Dick Inglima

I was born in Brooklyn in 1925. We were poor, like everybody else, but my dad always had a job, so we managed to get through the Depression okay. I didn't find out that Brooklyn was a slum until 1943, when I joined the Navy. I ended up at weather school in Lakehurst, New Jersey, and from there I was transferred to the Alameda Naval Air Station in California. The day we arrived, the commander told me and my buddies George and Joe that if we played ball with him he'd fix it so that we'd never have to see the war. We volunteered to get into the fleet anyway. We were just kids; we didn't know what we were getting into.

I was assigned to the *Intrepid*, an Essex-class aircraft carrier that was a prime target for the Japanese kamikazes. They really wanted to stop us. When I was 19, we got hit real bad and a lot of my friends were killed. We limped into San Francisco and everyone got leave. Being back in New York was one of the most depressing times of my life. My folks got a telegram that my brother had been shot down and was missing in action. The Battle of the Bulge was going on, and there'd just been the Malmedy Massacre.

My brother turned up okay and I got sent back to the Pacific for more kamikaze action. Near the end of the war I got tired of that and put in for a transfer. I was sent to Waipeo Training Base on Oahu, where I reunited with my buddy, George Paul. He and I started getting interested in going to Alaska, especially when we found out there was a university in Fairbanks. We went there in July of 1945.

I met Lynn Morris at UAF and we fell madly in love. We were married in May of 1946 and moved to Seldovia, where her family lived. Things were really poor in Seldovia then. Salmon was all depleted, everybody was robbing the streams, and they were still using traps, fishing 24 hours a day. Lynn worked for her folks in their grocery store, Morris and Morris. I went to work for Squeaky Anderson as a machinist's helper. I also went halibut fishing and seining.

For a while we lived in Spokane, Washington so I could attend Gonzaga University. Our first child, Diane, was born there. Then we went to New York, where I finished my schooling. Our second child, Dickie, was born in Brooklyn.

We went back to Seldovia and one day I got a call from a friend who worked for the Corps of Engineers, asking me if I wanted a job. So we relocated to Anchorage for four years. When Lyni was born, Lynn went back to Seldovia with the kids, so her mother could help her. Lynn's dad was getting pretty old and he needed someone to run his business, so I quit the Corps and we moved back to Seldovia on Thanksgiving Day, 1954.

I ended up buying the business and right about then things started picking up in Seldovia. They started fishing king crab. Then shrimp hit. Then salmon started to pick up. Our fifth child, Helyn, was born in 1955.

Seldovia was like no other place I've ever known. It was a way of life. People that we knew, we gave them a key to the store so they could come

Dick Inglima joined the Navy at age 17

in at their convenience to get groceries. They'd just write it down. In 1956 I was elected to the city council on a write-in ballot. I was on the council for ten years, then I became mayor.

Nobody had cars in the old days. People had sleds and four-wheel, flatbed carts and there was one little tractor that delivered groceries along the boardwalk. During the day Seldovia was slow, so my boys and I would go fishing. We built a new store, which opened in January of 1964. Two months later the earthquake hit. All the counters in the store faced north and south and when the quake hit they just kept rocking and rocking, but only one or two things fell off. We could hardly believe it.

We got word via radio that a lot of people had died in Anchorage, that Seward was burning, that Kodiak was completely gone. We couldn't get any real news; everything was exaggerated. They said there was a big tsunami coming and we should all get up to the school, which is what the whole town did. The bay was just like a whirlpool, the tide was coming in one way and going out the other way. It wiped out the boat harbor, all the boats; it just took everything out.

The army flew in 10,000 sandbags and we bagged the whole boardwalk, from one end of town to the other, all within a day's time. Pretty soon the urban renewal people came in with a lot of money, offering everybody loans to rebuild their houses. But the canneries decided to relocate to Kodiak, and there was an exodus out of Seldovia.

I was against urban renewal from the start and within a period of six months our lives totally changed. We'd been riding high and now we were almost destitute, so in '66 I resigned as mayor and we moved to Homer. We went from living in a big, beautiful home, the one Lynn had grown up in, to a portion of Mrs. Walli's little store, which we had bought. Eventually we built a new store and gradually we got back on our feet. Whether we were living in Seldovia or Homer, our house was always a hub. Our five kids would have their friends over; the house was always full. Life in Homer was a lot different than in Seldovia. We got a car; we could go to Anchorage anytime we wanted. Things were good, and Lynn said that leaving Seldovia was the best thing we could have done.

I lost my wonderful Lynn in 1992 and nothing has been the same since. But I keep busy. I've been on many different boards. I travel. Lynn and I had some hardships, but they brought us closer together. We were really lucky. All five of our kids stayed in Alaska, and we always had lots of real good friends. That was important to us.

Mary Oldham

Mary Oldham came to Alaska in 1958. A young bride and new mother, she and her family settled in Anchorage, where she taught school for several years on the base at Elmendorf. When her husband decided he'd had enough of Alaska, Mary decided she hadn't. She kept her job and gravitated toward what seems to be the life she was born for: adventure.

Mary and Kris Oldham on the airstrip at High Lake Lodge, 1971

While I was teaching in Anchorage, there were three of us, all women, all co-workers, who decided we wanted to learn to fly. We joined the Seven Star Flying Club and flew on weekends, taking turns, an hour at a time. I couldn't afford to continue my flying lessons, so I was lucky when an instructor asked me to haul some big loads of canned goods to the Nebesna River. That meant hours on my log book, plus he was paying for the gas. I'd take off from Merrill Field just as heavy as could be. I had minimum gas and had to land in Gulkana for fuel, then continue to the base of the Nebesna Glacier.

When the camp owner found out that I'd hunted with my dad as a child and that I could do a lot of things that women didn't traditionally do in those days, he asked me, "Would you like to cook in my camp?" So I cooked that summer and went back to teaching when school started in the fall. The next year he wanted me to be the go-fer. He had an air taxi operation and frequently flew miners to various places. That was a lot more exciting than cooking, and I was gaining experience as a pilot.

Soon thereafter I married Ken Oldham, who was well known even then as a pilot and guide. We had an air taxi service out of Merrill Field and eventually decided that, with our collective experience, it might make sense to build a hunting and fishing lodge. This was in 1961. The spot we settled on was about 50 miles north-west of Talkeetna, at a place we named High Lake. It was on the side of a mountain, at about 2600 feet. We could look down across the Susitna Valley, into the Stephan Lake depression, and over toward the Talkeetna Mountains. It was absolutely spectacular.

There was nothing there, not even a road, and there never could be; everything had to be brought in by air. We flew in every brick and board. The only exceptions were a track vehicle and a Caterpillar, which we had to have to make our runway. We also packed in horses and a pack mule. Ken and I cleared the land, and the men we hired as guides in the fall came up and helped set up camp.

We chose that particular area because it was rich in game animals and because it was so inaccessible. We knew that, by judiciously taking careful hunting precautions, we would have a sustainable hunting environment. We started getting clients when it was still a tent camp. Most of them were European, and a few came from the southern U.S. It took a couple of years to get the lodge built, and that winter the whole family moved in. We had a big Ashley stove and lots of wood to burn, and we just kind of cozied in for the season. To me it was ideal. We had lots of time to read and teach the children what we knew.

We continued with our goal of establishing a first class lodge: fine wines, linen tablecloths, china and crystal. Our clients were so supportive, we unofficially named several mountain peaks in their honor. Our pattern was that we lived for nine months a year at High Lake, and three months each winter in Kotzebue. For the 11 years we had the lodge, we home-schooled our children. We'd receive boxes and boxes of books and equipment. I can't say enough good things about home schooling; I really believe in it. Later on it did get complicated because we had one child in high school and one in kindergarten and two in between. They all did extremely well, though.

Every so often we brought the children to Anchorage for their medical checkups and shots and a chance to see the big city. We were well aware that they were growing up without television and the other trappings of modern life. We had a wonderful collection of records and listened to music all the time. The children grew to be familiar with classical music because that's what I liked, and Ken preferred Broadway show tunes, so that's what they got.

We were living at the lodge when our youngest child was expected. I'd been flying back and forth for checkups and at a certain point the doctors told me I really should stay in town. I told them I couldn't. I had a business to run and I had to get back to the lodge; we had a big hunting party coming in. I did promise, however, that I'd come back as soon as the hunters left. Ken went to Anchorage to pick up the group, leaving one plane and one nervous bachelor pilot, Mike Fisher. Then my water broke and I realized I wasn't going to have this baby on schedule; he was not going to wait until it was convenient for me. By then it was dark and a storm was raging. I told Mike, "We're not going to take this Super Cub through the mountains on a dark and stormy night. We're going to have this baby right here. This is my fourth child and I think I can do it."

There was only one other woman there, the cook. She was married but had never had any children and she was pretty concerned about the whole situation. I told her to get some water heated, to do the water thing. I kept thinking, I must have made a bad decision somewhere along the line or this wouldn't have happened.

When dawn broke the weather was clear, so I got a pile of towels and put them on the back seat of the plane. Mike, very apprehensive, flew me to Anchorage. We were all familiar with the fact that Don Sheldon had delivered a baby in his Super Cub and that it was a huge mess. I was determined not to have that happen, and it didn't. We made it to Anchorage and Kris was born in the old hospital on 9th and L.

Wolves were a real problem for us at High Lake. The area we lived in had probably less than 6% calf survival in the moose crop. That was quite a concern, trying to keep enough moose there to support the homesteaders. We had some large wolf packs, one of which was about a mile and a half away.

Mary Oldham with a polar bear shot on the Chukchi Sea

It's very hard to live near a pack of 35 wolves because they're hungry just about all the time. We had not only the children to worry about; we had horses too, and a dog of course. We were often visited by the fish and game agents, who were forever trying to figure out what to do. There was a bounty on wolves, so one of the ways we made money in the winter was that Ken would shoot wolves. The bounty was $50 apiece, plus you could sell the hide.

On one particular wolf hunt my husband and five-year-old son didn't return when they should have. It kept getting later and later, and finally it was totally dark. The weather was about 20 below. I was able to stay fairly calm; I figured everything would work out okay. But I was constantly running back and forth between the main building, where the other three children were, and the building where the HF radio was located. Occasionally one of the kids would ask, "Where's Daddy?" I didn't know what to say.

When he hunted, Ken was usually home within three hours, so I knew fairly soon that something had gone wrong. I continued trying to radio him, but those old HF radios weren't very reliable and I was never able to reach him. As the evening progressed, the bush pilots from Talkeetna took to the air, searching for the two of them. There was a full moon and they were looking for a signal.

I'm not one to panic. Ken was an excellent pilot, they were properly dressed, and of course they had survival gear. But nevertheless, to be out of contact for almost

15 hours; that was a little tough. I could pick up radio station KHAR in Anchorage, and they kept announcing, "Famous bush pilot Ken Oldham and his son are down in the Talkeetnas." I have to admit that hearing that over and over put me a little on edge.

Later on, Ken told me that, after shooting one wolf, they decided to land. The snow had covered up a small berm, which broke the gear under one side of the airplane. It was the type of accident that doesn't happen very often for someone as skilled as Ken. He tried unsuccessfully to radio me, and finally reached someone in Talkeetna on their HF radio. He only sent one message because he was afraid that if he kept trying, he'd run his battery down and be unable to guide the pilots in when they did start searching.

The message he relayed was that he was near Cliff Hudson's trapping cabin. The comical thing about that was, Cliff had lots of trapping cabins, and he was the only one who knew where they were. Ken's plan was that the two of them would walk to the cabin the next day if nobody found them. I think it was Don Sheldon who finally spotted them. He was giving radio commentary on HF radio, which was relayed to Anchorage, and I was listening to it third hand over KHAR. Finally they called to tell me they were both okay, and Cliff Hudson went in to pick them up.

It wasn't much of an adventure for them. They had wrapped up in the sleeping bag and cozied into the airplane out of the wind, so they were warm and comfy. They had some kind of candy and a can of fresh peaches, which gave them juice and sugar. Canned peaches were very important to fliers in those days. By that time I had lived through a lot of adventures myself, so this was just one more thing, but I was awfully glad when they returned home.

One time some friends flew to the lodge to visit us. They landed short and nosed their airplane up. The pilot's wife was sitting in the back of the Super Cub, and when her head went forward she scalped herself on a piece of metal. I ran out and they were just sitting there, both in shock, almost knocked out. The door was locked from the inside; there wasn't any way to get it open. The header tank was dripping gasoline and I couldn't see if the master switch was on, so I figured there could well be an explosion.

I still can't believe I did this, but somehow I managed to tear the door of that Super Cub right off. I could get my fingers around the front piece of it, and I just ripped it off. The wife was still pretty well out and, because she was blinded by the blood, she couldn't see to undo her seat belt. Her husband was leaned forward; I figured

I'd deal with him later. I took her away from the airplane as far as I could and went back and pulled him out. By then he was able to walk a little.

While he dealt with the airplane, I walked her up to the house. I discovered that an Ace bandage worked very well for keeping a scalp on, plus it pretty much stopped the bleeding, though it didn't do much for shock. But we had warm blankets, and pretty soon some people came in on a float plane and took her to Providence Hospital in Anchorage.

Once I loaned my airplane to another guide and outfitter in Kotzebue, and somewhere in his flying he knocked the tail wheel off. For the flight back to High Lake, Ken tied on a stick and told me it was crucial to get the power up, not to let the tail drag, or it would bounce all over the place and wreck the plane.

We left Kotzebue in two planes, landed in Galena, then took off on the airstrip which used to be on the frozen Yukon, headed for High Lake. Our route was across the northern part of Minchumina Lake and through Anderson Pass, just to the north of Denali. The winds were quite severe from the west and when we went through the pass I was too low. I got caught in the downdraft and it pushed me over a cliff. I dropped over a thousand feet in a matter of a few seconds.

Ken, who could see what had happened, radioed me, saying "Climb up! Climb up!" But you can't climb out of something like that or you'll lose lift. I knew that if I put the nose down and increased the speed I might be able to zoom out of it, under the draft. So that's what I did. I gunned it and tried to keep out of the treetops. It was pretty scary, but since my son was in the back seat, I didn't fool around, and we made it okay.

We often had people coming in to make films, and they'd hire us to do the support work. On one occasion we were up the Noatak River in the Brooks Range, preparing to shoot a scene involving a grizzly bear. When we located one, the whole crew got ready. The heroine was safe and sound back in Hollywood and I was her stand-in. They had me all dolled up, and I was to walk out onto this space with the bear.

There were people all around, and the bear must have felt cornered. Since I was coming toward him, he came toward me. I was being "backed up" by Kenny Westenbarger, a great hunter. I was trying to do what the script called for, but when the bear got too close, Kenny had to shoot it. But it didn't die; it was still coming. I thought, this is it. I knew better than to do this. At the last second, Kenny fired another shot and the bear died on the front of my snowshoes. I still remember those little beady red eyes. That was probably the scariest moment in my life, and the most foolish thing I've ever done. I learned a good lesson from it, though: if you feel something is wrong, don't do it.

To pass the time during the winters, I wrote several articles for Alaska Magazine. I also wrote a book, *Farewell, Nanook,* trying to inform people about the possible ramifications of the Native Claims Settlement Act. I felt that it was a really crucial thing for the Natives - that they could have lost everything. Fortunately, it didn't turn out that way.

The way our family lived was unique, no doubt about that. Some people would say we lived dangerously. We felt we were learning to live with nature, trying to understand it well enough so that it didn't get the better of us. One time a man landed his float plane at High Lake. We had a large green grass lawn that you could see from four or five thousand feet. It was Kentucky bluegrass, not the color of the rest of the world around there. Once you saw it, you could see the buildings and the runway. This man landed his plane and when he stepped out, he asked, "What is this, Shangri-La?"

Olga Hilleary

My mother was of Russian Aleut descent, born in Ninilchik to the Oskolkoff lineage. My father was of Norwegian, Russian and Irish descent; he was born into a large family in Kodiak, the Mahles. My mother had been married before she met my father, so my family is a mixture of half-siblings.

I was born in 1927 at the railroad hospital in Anchorage. My father worked for the railroad as a crane operator when Anchorage was still a tent city. When I was three, my mother died. Left with a large family of small children, my father had to decide how to raise us. He sent the three youngest - me and my brothers, Paul and Harold - by train to the government mission school, St. Marks, in Nenana. The next three in age were sent to another government school in Eklutna. The rest were old enough to be on their own.

I lived at the school in Nenana for the next 12 years. The school was situated one mile from the town, along the banks of the Nenana River. The mission school was a two-story building with a full basement and an attic. There were maybe 35 to 40 children there at any one time, ranging in age from five to 19. The children were mostly from villages along the river or in the Interior.

There was a small staff of teachers, all from the New England states. Several of them I remember most fondly. Bishop John Bentley, the headmaster, lived nearby with his wife in a beautiful log cabin. He eventually became the bishop of the entire diocese of Alaska. The head matron was Bessie B. Blacknell, a pleasant, kindhearted and very capable woman. She was extremely fun-loving, but firm when necessary.

Our deaconess, Ann Kathleen Thompson, took charge of the nursing responsibilities, along with her many other duties. She taught all eight grades in our one-room schoolhouse. She was a mentor to me, encouraging me to read and teaching me to use the sewing machine, an old Singer treadle machine. I will always have fond memories of her.

St. Marks was a very poor, frugal place. We grew our own vegetables and had a root cellar to keep crops through the winter. We were fortunate to have a wonderful handyman, Fred Miller. He lived in Nenana with his wife and children. He was a jack-of-all trades and could maintain, build, or repair anything. He took my oldest brother under his wing and taught him to be his right-hand man.

In the summers we girls tended the vegetable gardens and the boys tended the fishwheels. They also cleaned fish for winter food for the 10 huskies the school kept for working dogs. After their day at school, Mr. Miller would take the boys across the river to cut wood for the furnace and wood cook stove. They would then haul it by hand or by dog-team for future use.

We were never allowed to walk to town without an adult chaperone. It was only a mile, but it seemed like a long way to me. When I was younger, it was a thrill for me to go downtown to the railroad station, to watch the train pull up and see the passengers come and go. In the summers we were allowed to go watch the big sternwheelers come up the river, carrying both freight and passengers. We'd have dances most Friday evenings. The general public was allowed, but they seldom came, so we danced among ourselves to the music of a wind-up phonograph.

When four us were ready for high-school, a small addition was built on the back of the grade school, and Father Krone became our teacher. The next year my friend, Bessie, and I walked to Nenana to attend school, which was a long frigid walk most days. In all those years I was very close to my two brothers, but I always dreamed of the day I could go back home and be reunited with the rest of my family. I hadn't heard from any of them during the 12 years I was away.

A lot of the kids were from the local area, so their families would come to visit. When I was very young, I would pretend that someone was coming to see me. I'd run outside and down the road to meet my pretend visitor. Of course, no one ever came, and I decided that when I grew up I would have a large family of my own.

I left Nenana in the spring of 1945. We learned that help was needed at the Palmer Hospital, so I worked there in the TB ward that summer. While I was in Palmer, my sister, Ida, contacted me. Reuniting with my family had always been my highest priority, so instead of going back to St. Mark's, I moved in with another of my sisters, Doris, the family matriarch. She and her husband lived in Anchorage at 5th and A, in a home they rented from Russian Jack. Even though their house was small, the family gathered there on every occasion. It was like a dream come true, to be back with my family again.

At Doris's insistence, I began my junior year at Anchorage High School, but I only stayed one semester, to my later regret. Instead, I chose to go to work at Providence Hospital, on 9th and L. Back then they had rooms in the basement for the girls who worked there. We were all about the same age, so it was a lot of fun. I worked with a girl named Frankie. We worked on the second floor, which was the general patient area and the maternity wing. We cleaned and served trays to all the patients. It was hard work but we enjoyed it. On weekends we went to dances, usually at the USO. We loved dancing to big band music. On my days off I visited with my family.

Bessie Blackwell mends 8-year-old Olga's pants, 1935

In 1948 I married Walter Nygard, a longtime friend of my brothers. Our daughter, Jeannie, was born toward the end of the year in Anchorage. Unfortunately, our marriage was short-lived. Walter was killed in a small plane crash, flying to Skwentna on a beautiful spring day to see my oldest brother, Clarence, who was trapping there.

My second husband was also a family friend, Isam Hilleary. He was born in Kenai of Russian Aleut descent. We were married in Anchorage in 1951. We had five more children, who were like stair-steps in age: Richard, Debra, Pamela,

Ronald and Russel. We bought a home in Rogers Park, back when it was way out of town. It was a nice neighborhood and I'd have been happy to stay there forever. But Isam's roots were in Kenai, where his father owned property. So, after commuting to our fish camp on the Kenai Peninsula every summer for several years, we decided to move to North Kenai.

Isam built our home whenever there was a lull in fishing in 1963. It was unfinished when we moved in, but it was good to be in our own home, as we had been renting a very small cabin. The isolation was difficult for me at first. We had no nearby neighbors, and it was a completely different lifestyle from the city, where I could pick up the phone and talk to my family, or jump in the car and go visit them. But, as the years passed, I learned to love being a homesteader, and now I wouldn't dream of living anywhere else.

Isam knew Cook Inlet like the back of his hand, having fished from the time he was nine years old. He was Alaskan through and through. He loved to hunt and fish. He built his own wooden boats in the early years, before switching to aluminum dories. He was a commercial setnet fisherman at East Forelands, and for many years I fished by his side.

I was scared to death of the water but, as long as Isam was the skipper, I felt safe. I'd put on my hip boots and do everything he did. In those days we still used wooden corks and linen nets. We had two huge wooden barrels; one had bluestone disinfectant to wash the nets; the other was for rinsing. Every spring we had to chip the old paint from the wooden dories and wooden buoy kegs and repaint them, plus hang and mend the nets. It was hard, intense work but we loved it. We spent our summers on the beach, at the same spot where our family still fishes today. Everyone pitched in, and it was a wonderful place to raise children.

My only regret is that I never finished high school, as it could have opened many doors for me. Later I did go back and get my GED, and I've taken some college classes throughout the years to broaden my education.

Isam was a wonderful father and grandfather. He died in 1993. Though he is no longer with us, my children and I are still very close. All except one daughter live within a few miles from me, and they all have lovely families. I now have 12 grandchildren and two great-grandchildren. So, you see, I did end up with that big family I always yearned for.

Irvin Evenson

Mildred and Irvin Evenson have one of those to-die-for views. Hardly a man-made thing in sight, just mountains and trees and the lovely Kasilof River. Located off Kalifornsky Beach Road, I had driven past the Evensons' place dozens of times and never seen it. It's invisible from the road. As you motor past, you'd never guess that just a few hundred feet away, such a glorious view is even possible.

You only have to spend a couple of hours with Mildred and Irv Evenson to know, they're about the happiest couple around. Though he's 87 and she's 82, you'd never peg them as octogenarians. They travel all over the world. Their young grandchildren frequently drop in to play. Margaritas and nachos are high on their favorite food list. And to make sure they stay warm in the winter, they spend a few months in Texas each year.

I commend them for their youthfulness and Mildred hastens to inform me: in 1995 Irv was the Texas state champion shuffleboard player. When I tell Irv, "Not too shabby for an old guy," he beams with pride.

I was born in Wisconsin in 1914. In 1934 I was working in a CCC camp, making about 15 cents an hour, when President Roosevelt okayed the plan to send a few hundred Midwestern families to Alaska, to homestead the area around Palmer. They needed workers, so some friends of mine went up there to check it out. Right away they wrote to me, saying I should come up as fast as I could, that the wages were 60 cents an hour. And that's just what I did, I got here as quick as I could. We helped set up tents, clear land and build homes for the colonists.

I decided to take a little vacation from that in 1939. I went to the World's Fair in

San Francisco, then to visit my folks in northern Wisconsin. While I was there I met Mildred Cox. She was really something, an adventurous kind of girl, and I convinced her that she just might like living in Alaska.

I came back that summer and started working on the base at Elmendorf, pouring concrete seven days a week. Mildred was planning to join me in September and, since there wasn't a blasted place in town to be had, I had to get started building a house. I had some property on 10th, between Denali and Eagle, so I moved out of the boarding house where I'd been staying and put up a tent on the land. After I got off work each night, I'd go to work on the house. There were lots of people living in tents at that time. You could hear hammering all night long. In the summers, that's when you really heard it.

Mildred arrived in early September and we got married right away. We spent a couple of luxurious days in a hotel then moved into the tent. It was a real wet fall that year, and it got pretty cold when winter set in. Finally, on the 11th of November, we got enough of the house built that we could move in.

In 1943 we decided to get out of Anchorage. We bought 40 acres out in Sand Lake, seven miles away, where there were just a handful of homesteaders. We bought a little 12' by 20' cabin, put skids under it, and hired a guy with a Cat to drag it out there. Pretty soon we got the chance to buy the 80 acres next to us, and we ended up living there for 25 years, raising potatoes.

I'd never been a farmer, but everybody knows that potatoes are a good crop in Alaska. I was able to make a living at it 'cause I built a big storage unit and had it refrig-

The Evenson family farmed potatoes in the Sand Lake area for 25 years.

Mildred Evenson displays her Anchorage produce, 1941

erated. I could dig my potatoes in September, keep most of 'em, and sell 'em in June, July and August the following summer, when nobody else had potatoes. Most of our crop went to the military. I'd deliver 'em to Elmendorf and Fort Rich, then they'd fly 'em to all the military bases. Floating around the country yet are lots and lots of 10-pound and 15-pound mesh bags that say "Evenson's Sand Lake Potatoes."

The potato business was good to us. We had three boys, so it was a family operation. We only had to hire one guy, to help grade potatoes in the winter. Mildred was half of the crew that cut all the seed potatoes in the spring. She was the field boss when we were digging, and the grader when we sorted, which was all winter long. She looked at millions of potatoes and never had a batch turned down by the inspector.

We'd sometimes get an order for 30 or 40 tons and have to get 'em all ready. The inspector from Palmer would come, he'd have the right to open any bag, or as many as he wanted, to inspect for quality. In all those years we never had one bit of trouble. I always said it was because of Mildred. She had good eyes and fast fingers.

In 1968 we got tired of being potato farmers. We moved down to Kenai, bought a fishing boat, and I became a commercial fisherman. We already had a little spot there, on the bluff overlooking the water, where we'd built a cabin in '64. The big earthquake caused all that land along the bluff to drop, and those winter storms would really beat on the bank. Within two years, we had to move the cabin back. Two years later we were going to have to move it back again. So I got in my airplane and flew around, looking for a place to live.

I found a great spot and thought, if I can just find out who owns this piece of property, maybe I'll get lucky and he'll want to sell. I went to the land office and it turned out the guy was delinquent in his mortgage and just tickled to death to sell it, so I bought a hundred acres. We got the cabin from the beach, brought it over here and lived in it for five years, 'til I got around to building a house. Eventually all three of our sons, Dick, Bob and Dan, and their families, moved down here too.

When I bought my airplane, part of the deal was that they threw in some flying lessons, so that really appealed to me. I ended up building an airstrip, since we had all that property in Sand Lake, and I was able to keep my plane at home. When we came down to the Kenai, I cleared a strip here too.

I loved flying, but when I got to be 75, I said to myself, you're a little too old to fly, you'd better quit before you get up there and forget something important. Besides, I'd looked down on the backs of enough moose and bear, and I didn't need to do it anymore. But I've still got my plane; it's just as good as new. One of my sons owns it now.

Bill Bacus

I was born in Vancouver, B.C. in 1916. My dad had property in the little town of Point Roberts, right on the U.S.-Canadian border. In those days you had the option of being a citizen of either country, so I chose to be an American.

The Navy's first CB

I went through school, then moved down to Vallejo, where I joined the carpenter's local as an apprentice. I worked in the shipyards and eventually got to be a pile driver.

Then the war broke out. I was just the right age to be drafted; in fact, the draft board was sending me notices every week. I knew I had to do something, and I sure didn't want to go into the Army. By accident I saw a notice in the paper that said the Navy was looking for construction workers, so I took a bus to San Diego and talked to them. They were putting together a new group called CBs (Construction Battalion) and they seemed real interested in me. They told me to come back in a few days, on the 6th of February ('42), when they would begin taking enlistments. They put me on their list and I said, "See you in a few days."

When I got home, there was my draft notice. I'd been inducted into the U. S. Army and was supposed to report to fort so-and-so on a particular day. I didn't know what to do, so I got on the bus again and went back to the Navy recruiting office in San Diego. I told them what had happened and that they'd have to take me off their list. The officer said, "I think you should talk to the commander." When the commander came to see me, he said, "I think we can help you out. Raise your right hand and repeat after me ..." And right then and there I was inducted into the Navy. That was the 5th of February, so I was the first CB. I don't know how they worked that out with the Army; all I know is, I never heard from them again.

After basic training, my battalion was sent to Rhode Island for a couple months, to a place near Quonset Point, where they make Quonset huts. They had a continual rotation, one battalion after another would go through, and they'd show you how to erect the hut and how to tear it down. It took us a month or so to do it, that first time. We had a barracks and a mess hall at Davisville; we'd go back and forth by bus every day to Quonset Point.

They attached some of us CBs to the Marines, so we were allowed to wear either uniform. When we went on liberty in Providence, if the girls liked sailors, we wore Navy uniforms, and if they liked Marines, we were Marines. After training in Rhode Island, our battalion spent a year and a half with the Marines in Pago Pago and Samoa. We'd go ashore and the Marines would leave while we stayed and put up the Quonset huts.

Eventually our guys started having health problems; they were dropping one by one, and there weren't any hospitals in Samoa. The Navy stepped in and said, no more duty in the South Pacific for you, and they shipped us to places with cold weather and no mosquitoes. That's when I got sent to Kodiak.

For years the Army had been building bases in Alaska, and in 1939 the Navy decided to build a big base up here. They went to a lot of trouble, figuring out where to put it. It had to have a deep harbor and it had to be a place that was fogged in all the time - the more fog the better - so the enemy couldn't locate us. They started looking for the foggiest place in Alaska. Dutch Harbor? Cold Bay? They had no idea, but they had the money. They turned the job over to the Army, and basically what they did was pair up two guys who got along and dropped them off at places all up and down the coast of Alaska. They gave them lots of gear - they were totally equipped - and their job was to keep a log of the weather every hour of every day for one year. When they looked at the results, they found out that Kodiak was the foggiest place in Alaska. That's why they built the base here.

Before the war, Kodiak was just a little fishing village. When the military came in, they pretty much took over the whole town. Civilians could stay if they wanted to, and the government gave passage on steamships to anybody who wanted to leave. There had been some private construction done on the base, but then the military took over and things got going in high gear.

We had at least five battalions on Kodiak. They built the base, the FAA towers, the bunkers, the missile site, everything. We had a special battalion that all they did was longshore. And of course we put up lots of Quonset huts. Pretty soon they were all over Alaska. Kodiak was a big base, lots of buildings, lots of personnel. We could hear the Japanese flying overhead but, with the blackouts and all that fog, they never could find us.

We had so many jobs for construction workers, you could pick any job you wanted. After being in Samoa, I thought Alaska was pretty cold, so I went to work in the powerhouse. There was a civilian in charge, and we only worked eight hours a day, so I spent one winter doing a real warm and soft job.

Like I say, people had the option to stay, but the town was nearly all military. There was no civilian fire department, no bank, no police, no hotel. There were lots of liquor stores though, so we had to have military police. You weren't allowed to leave the island when you were on liberty, so the bars were about the only places to go.

In the spring we had so many military personnel in town, they had to double the number of shore patrol. So I did that, drove people back and forth between the base and town. We had 26 taxi cabs and no dispatcher; one of the liquor stores became the dispatcher. We had to get everybody back to the base by midnight. It was another good job; we didn't have many problems. There were plenty of big guys to take care of any trouble-makers.

There was no fishing in Kodiak for the four years of the war. All the canneries had to close, just shut their doors. While I was on shore patrol, I got acquainted with all the cannery guys in town, and I knew they were looking toward a lot of work after the war.

When the canneries started opening up in 1946, they had lost contact with all the people from the Seattle area who had come up to work year after year, so they had to find new people. I was living in Bellingham then, and I started coming up to Kodiak each summer, working in the cannery. I put in four seasons, then I came up permanently in '49. I found work in Kodiak and rented a house, then I went down to Vancouver, B.C. and married the girl I'd been dating, Doris Wesley.

I spent the rest of my working career in construction. Just like the cannery guys said, there was lots of work in Kodiak, and I was in the right business at the right time. Just after we got Kodiak built, full of homes, a thriving community, the '64 tidal wave hit and we had another huge project to work on.

At the time of the earthquake I was working for the FAA, putting up antennas on Long Island, a short distance from Kodiak. Usually at 5:30 we'd have been on the water, coming back to town. But that day, since it was Good Friday, the skipper said, "Why don't we take off early tonight and go home?" By the time the wave hit, we were back in Kodiak, otherwise we'd have been caught in the middle of it. I had purchased a 10-unit motel near the waterfront in 1963 and just about had it up and running when the wave hit and washed it away.

Doris and I raised our three kids in Kodiak and each of them paid for their college education by running our fish sites. They'd come home for the summer and go to work; I think they enjoyed it. They'd bring their friends to fish too. There was always plenty to do. I retired 20 years ago, then started my own construction business. I have to say, Kodiak has been real good to us; we've lived here 53 years now and we don't have any plans to leave.

Mildred Mantle

I grew up on a farm in Minnesota. I taught elementary school for a while and worked at the University of Minnesota. In early 1941 my good friend, Henrietta "Penn" Swanson, decided she wanted to visit her brother Paul in Alaska. She was going to drive her car to Seattle, then put it on a steamship. Another gal and I decided to go with her.

Paul met us and took us to his little one-room shack - it had been a fox farm - on 5th and Gambell. He and his roommate moved into a tent and let the three of us have the building. It had two stories, and we slept in the unfinished upper room. In order to get into the sleeping area, we had to go outside and crawl up a ladder. We had to use several quilts to stay warm. There was a little wood-burning stove but it was in the room below. We had cold running water, a path to the outhouse, and we soon got used to taking saunas.

Before long we three girls moved out of the "Squeeze Inn," as we called it, and into a small duplex on 4th and A. It was a great life. We rarely locked our doors. Most people didn't have cars, but you felt safe taking a ride with anyone.

We had a piano in our new place. Someone from the military base suggested that we invite a few soldiers from the base over for Thanksgiving dinner. That was all right with us, and we invited the Air Corps quartet. After that the boys pretty much never left; they were there night and day. They'd come over and bring their friends, bring birthday cakes, bring no-occasion cakes. They told everybody, "Oh the girls would love to have you visit." We had a rule, and we were strict about it: no liquor. There was a clump of trees across the street from us. The ones who drank would stash their liquor there and run out every so often for a nip.

Last year my phone rang and a gentleman said, "This is a voice from your past, Ted Marcchi." He was one of the boys in the quartet, calling from Michigan. He said he'd just seen another one of the other "boys" a few days before. It was so great talking with him. We talked for a whole hour.

Here's a funny thing that happened. When people talk about the early days in Anchorage, they don't usually mention that many of the unmarried women in town

Mildred Mantle poses at Elmendorf Air Force Base for a bond drive, 1944

were prostitutes. The main house of prostitution was on C Street, not far from our house on A Street. One night a knock came on our door and a man's voice said, "Al the taxi driver sent me." I said, "All right, but what do you want?" He repeated that Al the taxi driver had sent him. I had no idea what he was talking about. When he repeated it the third time, he became very chagrined and said he must be at the wrong place. He hastily left.

The three of us had such fun. We loved Alaska right from the start. We had jobs and friends, but the main thing about Alaska was, there were so many opportunities. You were stretched beyond what you thought you could do. My first job was with the Corps of Engineers, helping with their reports. When the war broke out, the engineers were called into service, so I was told, "Well Mildred, you'll have to start doing the status of the construction on the base." "That's engineer's work," I said. "I can't do that!" They said, "Well you know it better than anyone else." So I'd go around and see what kind of progress the workers were making on all the buildings. I had never done anything like that, and only in Alaska could this happen.

Here's another funny thing. When the war broke out, the military started shipping all the wives home, and one of my jobs was to give out the slips for their evacuation. I was taking them around and I'll never forget, one man said, "Can I have two of those?"

After the war, I had a lot of annual leave coming. I had always wanted to work in a fish cannery, so I went to work at Libby's Cannery on the Kenai, waiting tables for a couple of months. While I was there, I got a wire from Noel Wennblom, the Anchorage District Attorney, asking me to meet him at the Kenai airport. Some burly seamen from the cannery took me upriver in a little skiff to the airport. That's where I met Mr. Wennblom, who offered me a job in his office. I have no idea how he heard of me, or why he would go to such lengths to locate me, but I ended up working in the DA's office.

That job was another big opportunity, a real stretch for me. Hearings were held in both the commissioners court and in the district court. One time the court reporter, a stenotype expert, had to take extended sick leave, and Judge Dimond ordered me into court to take the hearings, verbatim. I said, "I can't do that. I take shorthand." He said, "You can do it better than anyone else. You be in the court at 9:00 tomorrow morning." I was scared to death, but when you're forced to do things, you do them.

An interesting event took place while I was working for the DA's office. Three men had robbed a prominent madam in Kodiak. They stole her safe, took it outside of town and blasted it open. They were caught and brought to court in Anchorage, where they were released on bail. I had been in court, recording the hearing. Afterward, a friend and I were walking to a function out at Fort Richardson when a car pulled up and we were offered a ride. Naturally, we took it. Once we were inside, I realized that the driver was one of the Kodiak safe robbers. They dropped us off, no problem, but afterward, when I told my girlfriend, she almost fainted.

I met my husband, Hilton Mantle, a wonderful man, at the downtown ice skating rink. He was in the military at the time, and later worked for the Alaska Railroad. We were married in 1949. I worked in public relations for the Anchorage Chamber of Commerce for five years. The chamber's president, John Gorsuch, was also president of the Anchorage School Board. One day he said to me, "Mildred would you come to the school board meeting tonight and take notes?" I said I supposed I could. That lead to me being the school board secretary for 13 years, an evening job that I did in addition to my full-time day job.

My husband died in 1962 and I was in such a terrible state, I didn't know what to do. I even considered leaving Alaska, which would have been a serious mistake. Instead, I eventually sold our home and moved to Safehaven, a wonderful neighborhood on 11th Avenue. I also began working for the Anchorage Tuberculosis Association.

Later I worked at API for 13 years, as coordinator of hospital and community services. I was there at the very beginning, and it was a job I dearly loved. I organized the volunteer service department. I oversaw the patient's beauty shop and barber shop. I collected books and set up the library. I put out the newsletter, conducted tours and coordinated public and school education about the Institute. I've had a number of interesting jobs. I worked at the Anchorage Visitor's Association for a while, and also for the Anchorage Crippled Children's Association. All my work has been associated with public relations.

I've always loved riding my bicycle, and for a long time my goal was to ride a thousand miles each year. My friend, Janice, and I would meet and ride all over. I'd start in April and if I didn't ride 10 miles a day, I'd make it up later. I did that until four years ago. I've had the greatest life. I always felt as if I had come home when I arrived here. I once wrote a poem called *Alaska, The Great Land*, trying to sum up my feelings.

Alaska, The Great Land

It must have been the sixth day of the week

and God was genial with an artist's pride,

planning the final touches to His handiwork.

"Today I will create my masterpiece, the ultimate creation.

It will be immense, with soaring mountains

and untrammeled space, to stretch men's souls

and give them room to dream.

I'll pin there the lodestar of the Universe

and the bright spectrum of the Northern Lights

so that once visited, there will be no rest

until men's faces turn again to true north.

I'll make a land to hold them like a lover."

- Mildred Mantle
Anchorage, Alaska